The Significance of Prefixes in Sanskrit Philosophical Terminology

The Significance of Prefixes in Sanskrit Philosophical Terminology

Betty Heimann

PRINTWORLD
Publishers of Indian Traditions

Cataloging in Publication Data — DK
[Courtesy: D.K. Agencies (P) Ltd. <docinfo@dkagencies.com>]

Heimann, Betty, 1888-
The significance of prefixes in Sanskrit philosophical terminology / Betty Heimann.
p. cm.
Reprint.
Includes bibliographical references and index.
ISBN 13: 9788124606353

1. Sanskrit language — Suffixes and prefixes. I. Title.

DDC 491.2592 23

ISBN 13: 978-81-246-0635-3 ISBN 10: 81-246-0635-8
First published in 1951
Retypesetted and printed in India, 2012

Printed with the permission of the Royal Asiatic Society of Great Britain, London.

Published and printed by:
D.K. Printworld (P) Ltd.
Regd. Office : '*Vedaśrī*', F-395, Sudarshan Park
(Metro Station: Ramesh Nagar)
New Delhi - 110 015
Phones : (011) 2545 3975; 2546 6019; *Fax* : (011) 2546 5926
E-mail : indology@dkprintworld.com
Web : www.dkprintworld.com

Royal Asiatic Society Monographs
VOL. XXV

THE SIGNIFICANCE OF PREFIXES IN SANSKRIT PHILOSOPHICAL TERMINOLOGY

BY
BETTY HEIMANN, Ph.D., etc.

Printed and published under the patronage of
THE ROYAL ASIATIC SOCIETY

1951

Preface

I owe the idea for this book to my pupils.

It originated from the fact that they frequently proffered widely divergent renderings in my classes on Sanskrit philosophical texts and commentaries. Whenever they provided a translation which differed from the one I had myself in mind, I tried to trace the reason for our divergencies. It generally turned out that their translations were perfectly correct with regard to the dictionaries, but among the many lexicographical possibilities they had preferred to select those renderings which, as the most abstract and fixed, they considered the most appropriate for philosophical thought.

But there remains this problem : do all philosophical systems in all philosophical literature all over the world always employ the most abstract denominations? If this axiom does not hold good for Indian philosophical literature, then, in face of the embarrassing multitude of meanings proffered in the Western Sanskrit dictionaries, the primary task would be to trace the original meaning of each Sanskrit term and to separate it from its later divergent derivations. Not from any secondary meaning but from the concrete primary concept we have to try to find a connecting link to the meaning suggested by the context of the passage in hand.

From the very concreteness of Sanskrit linguistic expression there radiate widely divergent meanings, and more divergent meanings in fact than in any other Indo-European language.

The more dynamic the character of a language, the greater the impetus for such radiation, i.e. for divergency of the meanings derived. In the search for an adequate rendering of Sanskrit philosophical texts these principles have all to be kept in mind: the fundamental concreteness, the basic dynamics, the resultant ambiguity, and on top of it the necessary congruence of the term in question with the specific context in which it is introduced. These complex factors, their different valuation, or neglect of one of them, account for the great divergency of translations, i.e. interpretations.

The following essay tries to give a lead in the method of translating Sanskrit philosophical texts. It does not aim at providing a panacea for every difficulty of translation. On the contrary, it voices a warning not to overlook the basic complexity and oscillating ambiguity involved.

After having completed the following monograph in 1945, I was fortunate enough once more to spend some years of study and teaching in the East itself. It has taught me that also modern Eastern students have to be reminded of the creative nature of their languages and to revitalize their terminology. They, too, have consciously to revive their abstract and stagnant use of terms by retracing the meanings from the original productive and concrete roots.

Finally, a word of acknowledgement. The late Professor E. H. Johnston (Baliol, Oxford) was kind enough to read my MS. after its completion. He made various valuable suggestions. The passages concerned I have marked at their proper place in the footnotes.

Contents

1

Introduction

As I tried to point out in my "Deutung und Bedeutung indischer Terminologie" (*Proceedings of the International Congress of Orientalists*, Rome, 1935), fixation such as deadens fertile potentiality of meaning has always been repugnant to the Indian mind. In spite of all (late) systematics and predilections for classification India's terms never get the rigidness of Latin "termini", fixed limits. Hence I ventured in my "Terms *in statu nascendi* in the Bhagavadgītā"[1] to analyse the different means by which every term (noun) is revived in its functions. Either it is connected with its respective verbal root, with forms of its full verb, or its participles, or else its various potentialities are accentuated by putting it in a *tatpuruṣa-compound*, etc.

In this study then I shall approach the problem of the immanent changeability and dynamics of "terms" from yet another angle. The significance of prefixes, and preferably of prepositions used as prefixes, will be investigated. Dynamics is one of the leading Hindu notions, daily brought home by observations made in such a mainly tropical climate as that of India. Quickness of growth and decay can be observed in the fertile tropical districts of India (e.g. at the Malabar Coast and in Bengal), and an equally surprising quickness of change from barren desert during the period of drought to abundant fertility during the rainy season in the other regions of this

1. *New Indian Antiquary*, 1940.

subcontinent. Furthermore, the unbreakable regularity of sudden change from day to night with nearly no twilight, of growth and decay without the stages of slow budding and fading, led the Indian to concentrate on the dynamic aspect of life as manifested in continuous abruptness of change.

The reflection of these fundamental natural laws can be traced even in a field apparently as remote as grammar. In early discussions of the grammatical problems mirrored in Yāska's *Niruktam* there seems to have prevailed a tendency primarily to attribute the functional significance to the verb (*kriyā*, action!) of which the noun is considered only a derivative. From this fundamental assumption we may explain that Śākaṭāyana, quoted and refuted by Yāska (*Nir*. 1, 1, 3) came to the opinion that the secondary grammatical elements, like prepositions or prefixes, serve only the purpose of setting free the immanent divergent possibilities latent in the verb itself.

The basic problem in dealing with prefixes is their relation to the verbal roots to which they are attached. Three different views are taken of this. Either the prefixes are considered as *artha-vācaka*s, independent bearers of meaning. Or — and this is the more frequent attitude among the Indian grammarians — they are regarded as *artha-dyotaka*s, illuminants of the meaning immanent in the verb. This latter view is made clear by the simile of a lamp, the purpose of which is not self-illumination, but to throw light upon the actual shape and quality of the objects concerned, the verbs. A third school, with some difference of conception, regard the prefixes as *saha-kāriṇa*s, i.e. co-operants, with the verbs, respectively verbal nouns.[2] Yāska, in adopting the view of Śākaṭāyana's

2. This tripartition is still maintained in the late grammatical treatises, e.g. in Puṇyarāja's Comm. to Bhartṛhari's *Vākyapadīyam Kār*. 190.

opponent, Gārgya, asserts that the prefixes add their specific meanings to the dynamics of the verbal root to which they are attached. Hence, they are termed *upa-sarga*s, lit. the flowing (*sarga*) towards and upon (*upa*), thus providing an additional tendency.[3] The intentional forward motion expressed by the prefix *upa* is its primary meaning (cf. its general use, e.g. in *upa-cāra*, *upa-saraṇa*, and *upa-krama*, and further examples *passim* in my study), while the result of this motion towards an aim, the static meaning of *upa*, reaching this aim and nearness to it, is but its second, and thus secondary, significance.

As will appear below, I am inclined to emphasize that explanation of *upa-sarga* which attributes to the prefixes a definite independent tendency, i.e. a meaning of their own. In favour also of this view *Ṛgveda Prātiśākhya*s, 11, 5, may be quoted, where the prepositions (and prefixes) are plainly called *artha-vācaka*s, bearers of independent meanings. Their full functional tendency is furthermore enhanced by the teachings of Pāṇini, 1, 4, 59 ff. This past-master of Indian grammar attributes to "adnominal" prepositions, prefixes, and all other adverbial expressions like particles, etc. the significant term *gati*, motion. Whatever limits the activity of the verbal function to any particular direction serves to increase the intensity, as it were, of the sentence.

In the following studies, which have been made from the philosophical texts themselves, independently of the theories of Indian grammarians, I am bound to come to the conclusion that prepositions and prefixes in Hindu thought have retained

3. My explanation of the term *upa-sarga* originates from the mehod applied in the following expositions, but agrees on the whole with the orthodox view held by the Indian grammarians, cf. Durga's Comm. to *Niruktam*, p. 33, 1. 9 ff. : *ākhyātum upagṛhya arthaviśeṣam ime tasyaivo sṛjanti ity upasargāḥ*; similarly Puṇyarāja ad *Vākyapadīyam Kār.*, 192.

the motional and emotional significance which they apparently once had at the earliest stages of all languages. Paradoxically, it is through the very feeling of dynamics that the dynamics of prefixes seem periodically degraded by the Indian grammarians for the sake of giving full stress to the dynamical function of the verb. In the West, on the other hand, the concreteness of the prefixes has been effaced both, in theory and in practice, for the sake of logical abstraction; and this process has been favoured in the West by less dynamic conditions of nature in the temperate zone.

After these preliminary remarks the very problem of this essay has to be dealt with. Compound-terms of Hindu philosophical texts and the mental operations which are grammatically and philosophically expressed by the prefixes are to be examined. The noun to which a preposition is prefixed is thereby brought again into a dynamic condition or, if the simple noun is itself still pregnant with function, the prefix enhances and varies it according to its special tendency of direction. Here is a striking example for the directing power of prefixes in terms common to all Hindu philosophical systems and popular usage as well. The five life-winds, the *prāṇa*s, functioning in different directions throughout the human and animal body, are pregnantly formed with appropriate prefixes of motion connected with the verbal root *an*, to breathe. *Pr*(*a*)-*āṇa*, the respiration through the essential channels of breathing, forwards (*pra*) through nose and mouth; *ap*(*a*)-*āna*, the respiration which goes downwards away (*apa*); *sam-āna*, the central circulation (*sam*), which has its seat in the cavity of the navel; *ud-āna*, the breathing upwards out (*ut*), which rises up the throat and enters into the head, and *vy-āna*, that which is diffused (*vi*) through the whole body.

The prepositions are, so to speak, additional motors of the word to which they are applied. Even neutral verbal roots like *kar, dā, dhā, yā, yuj,* etc. obtain a specific sense by means of the prefixes added. A similar process, though not so distinctly developed, can be observed in ancient Greek, where a few, as it were, neutral roots can be made to take on a variety of meanings by application of prefixes. In Hindu philosophical thought, then, this fundamental law of dynamic expression is never lost sight of; not only the verbal form, not only the noun, not only the preposition, not only the adverb, but even the adjective which, in fact, is the least functional of them all, is still considered as active in function. *Yoga-sūtras*, 3, 17, and its commentary, expressly teach that even in terms like the "white palace" the function of "whitening" is still vividly felt.

Another significant discussion, bearing indirectly on this problem, is given in the commentary to *Yoga-sūtras*, 3, 26. Here the different proper-names for the seven hells are enumerated. They are all formed from the one basic noun *tala*, which is variated by prefixes, original prepositions or mere adverbs, the different hells being called : *pā-tāla, su-tala, vi-tala, a-tala, tal(a)-ātala*, etc. and thus all its immanent possibilities are traced from the one noun. This method of designation is a kind of *syād-vāda* of terms.[4] It would be worthwhile to investigate this characteristic Hindu law of formation of proper-names in a special study and to supplement from this angle of research my essay "Zur indischen Namenskunde" (*Festschrift Geiger*, 1931).

As to the present problem, merely a study of the variation of terms brought about by the application of prefixes is intended. Only those are considered which are to be found in the keywords of the different philosophical Sanskrit schools. Besides the philosophico-psychological gain for the single terms treated, it may result in some new orientation for the history of the Indian systems, their divisions, subdivisions, and

4. Cf. the Jainistic discussion of all possibilities of beings and my remarks on it pp. 69 f.

interconnections. In attempting to look at the different philosophical schools, not as regards their main tenets, but, so to speak, from outside, by investigating a linguistic, and apparently a minor, detail of word-formation, we gain a more objective and unbiased approach to them. Our Western clear-cut divisions of the six orthodox systems of Vedānta, Mīmāṁsā, Sāṁkhya, Yoga, Nyāya and Vaiśeṣika, and their combination in three dual systems, may turn out to be too rigidly fixed.A more elastic frame has to be found for giving account of the interconnection between the different groups and the dissociation within one and the same system which undoubtedly have taken place. The "isogloss" method may be extended to an "iso-systematic" research.

Already one student of mine, when tracing a special philosophical problem through the different systems,[5] produced an unexpected re-ordering of the interconnection of the systems, or at least of their subdivisions. Instead of the usual classification into the strictly divided orthodox "Six" or, at any rate, the orthodox "Three" double systems, he succeeded in establishing a new order under the headings Idealists, Realists, and Materialists. In this way he accounted for the separation of the Prabhākara and Kumārila schools within the Mīmāṁsā, and the Śaṅkara and Rāmānuja sects within the Vedānta. Besides, he was able to prove a closer connection between some of the Vedāntins and the Realists of the Nyāya-Vaiśeṣika type than with their transcendentalist brother-Vedāntins, etc.

This study, then, viewing the philosophical Indian systems not from a specific philosophical angle but from an outlook even more distant, that is a linguistic-psychological standpoint, is bound implicitly to reveal some more

5. Mr. S.K. Saksena in his thesis "The Nature of Consciousness in Hindu Philosophy", Benares, 1944.

unexpected views of relation and dissociation between the different philosophical schools.

As befits the character of such an investigation on a scarcely trodden path,[6] no completeness of research is striven after, but some remarks on principles only are intended. This essay on the significance of Sanskrit prefixes may provide a contribution to the study of Indian dynamics. Furthermore, it will throw into relief the epistemological ambiguity and super-logical elasticity characteristic of Indian thought.[7]

First, the innate dynamic meaning of the prefixes themselves is to be taken into consideration, irrespective of their application in the philosophical systems. After having traced the full meaning of each single prefix and its catalytic power — to use a chemical simile — on the noun to which it is added, we can apply it as a touchstone for the different philosophical schools. *Repulsion towards or predilection for certain prefixes, application of all or only of one shade of an ambiguous prefix within the different systems of philosophy is a sound criterion for the tendency followed by each philosophical school.*

To explain what is meant by this, some examples may be given: the concept of prefixes is based in India on her fundamental law of the prevalence of Space over Time (a

6. After having finished this essay I was glad to find that Mr. Kao Ming-K'ai, in his "Essai sur la valeur réelle des particules prépositionelles en chinois", Paris, 1940, has attacked the same problem of the significance of prefixes. Owing to the fact that the role of prefixes in Chinese is extremely individual and hardly to be applied to any other linguistic group, the author has treated the problem from quite another viewpoint and with a different method. But even so, his book provides a parallel to this study; Mr. Kao Ming-K'ai, too, has emphasized the dynamical aspect of prefixes and their uneffaced significance.

7. Cf. to this problem also my "Zur Psychologie der indischen Grammatik", *Archiv Orientální*, 1935.

significant example can be found in the *Uttarādhyāya*, S.B.E., xlv, p. 153).[8] Besides, as a careful study of the problem "Space and Time in Hindu thought" would easily demonstrate, nearly all significations of Time (e.g. *tatas, paścāt, agre, adhvan*, even *kāla* itself) are primarily designations of Space. The concreteness of Hindu thought is here prominent. It is a significant fact that the prefixes are hardly ever indications of concepts of Time, *uttara* obviously, and *pūrva* most probably, belong originally to the sphere of spatial conceptions. All the other prepositions, used as prefixes, are definitely derived from spatial movements. They are true *gati*s, motions *Sam, vi, ā, upa, pra, anu, prati, ati*, etc. mark directions, motions and place. Within the spatial range they designate, as I shall show later on in greater detail, differences in direction, extension and intensity. The latter makes a psychological research necessary besides a merely philological study. Prefixes which tend to the same direction, like *upa, pra*, and *ā*, though all designating the horizontal forward movement, are differentiated in their meanings according to intensity and intention. *Ā*, for instance, will turn out in the course of our investigation as indicating a quasi-mechanical general forward or occasionally backward motion,[9] while *upa* and in lesser degree[10] *pra* refer to a more intentional, and thus more intensive but less extensive movement. The same variations can be laid bare in the prefixes

8. The argumentation quoted above (aphorisms 6 ff.) asserts the superiority of Space on the grounds of its essential qualities of being unique and basic to all. It runs as follows : "Space is a unique substance (together with *dharma* and *adharma* and their qualities of motion and rest), while Time (together with Matter and souls) consists of an infinite number of substances. Furthermore, Space (*nabhas*) contains in itself all other substances, i.e. it provides room (*avagraha*) for all the other substances."

9. Cf., e.g. *ā-gantuka*, straying forward.

10. Cf. *pra-kāśa*, emitting light.

which designate dispersion in spatial directions. While *vi* expresses a kind of mechanical dissemination, *nis* (*nir*) represents a more emotional, as it were, an explosive act of dispersion.

On the other hand, there are groups of prefixes which correspond to each other as counterparts, e.g. *sam* and *vi*.

More characteristic, however, for specific Hindu thought are those prefixes which like *prati* have in themselves a meaning of counter-tension; *prati* implies the simultaneous forward and backward motion.[11]

Furthermore, the prefix *ati* holds a singular position; it is a kind of transcendental prefix ("beyond the limits"), and as such has its proper place in terms of Hindu metaphysics.

Besides, some of the prefixes, like *sam* and *vi*, embrace within themselves various spheres of meaning; *sam* is ontologically extensive, psychologically intensive; logically comprehensive. *Vi*, on the other hand, indicates separation and diversion, either as the final aim of separation between Matter and Spirit in the dualistic Sāṁkhya, or as the empirical fact of multiplicity or as discrimination in the realistic systems of Nyāya-Vaiśeṣika, or in an epistemological sense : ambiguity and a logical lack of definition.

From yet another angle we have to pay special attention to those prefixes which are more definite, because of their invariability of meaning. For instance, the prefix *ni* simply designates the direction from above, the fixing-down to one point. As such, *ni* has only a limited range of applicability. It is in general use in a few systems only; in others it is adequate merely for a special stage of development. *Ni*, the fixing-down,

11. Cf. my "*Polarity of the Indefinite*", Coomaraswamy Jubilee Volume, 1938, and my "Plurality, Polarity, and Unity in Hindu Thought", *Bulletin of the School of Oriental Studies*, 1939.

has its proper place throughout the Nyāya (*ny-āya*), which is based on the surveying order of the human mind, which settles and defines the objects by means of its superior reasoning. Besides, *ni* is appropriate for designating such terms of the Yoga system, as are concerned with one Yogic stage, that of fixation.

Accordingly, the prefix *anu*, along, i.e. following a formerly recognized path, has a very limited sphere of application in those systems which, like the Yoga, are based on the idea of successive and progressive stages of development. In the Nyāya system, however, *anu* shows a wider range of possibilities. Here deductions are made from former empirical perception. *Anu* is logically always something secondary. *Anu-māna*, inference, is a resuming of former direct impressions and judgements, it is the logical application, while *anu-bhava*, recognition, refers to psychological adaptation of a pre-established truth from without.[12]

Thus, as to our present problem, if we can rightly consider the prefixes, or the terms formed with these prefixes, as indicators of the respective tendencies of the classical systems of Indian philosophy, we may derive our conclusions from considerations of four facets of this problem : the fact which prefixes are preferred in the keywords of the respective systems, which are avoided, which are applied in one of their possible meanings only, and which, finally, if they are not ambiguous in themselves, are used in the various schools for terms of depreciation or appreciation. Examples hereof will be given in the later chapters.

---

12. A most instructive example of the significance of the prefixes *anu* and *vi* is shown in *Kāṭhaka-Upaniṣad*, 5, 15: "*tam eva bhāntam anu-bhāti sarvam, tasya bhāsā sarvam idam vi-bhāti.*" After (or through) Him (the *Ātman-Brahman*) who (truly) shines, everything shines; through His light the whole world shines everywhere.

The prefixes throw into relief, by the different modes of their application, the specific bent of the systems themselves.

There is yet another variant of this very problem to be examined while one studies the application of prefixes in the different Hindu philosophical schools. Not only the prefixes alone but their juxtaposition with a certain noun or verb has to be considered with regard to the general tendency of each system; for instance, the term *ā-bhāsa,* as compound, can have a positive or negative import. *Ā-bhāsa,* receptive reflection, is welcome in the Yoga system, which aims at making Man a mere receptacle of higher vision. The same, though with a slightly different significance, is the case in the Vedānta, which proclaims that Man is, and can never be more, than a reflection of the transcendental *Summum.* In the Nyāya, on the other hand, which is based on the acknowledgement of the independence of human reasoning, *ā-bhāsa,* the merely receptive reflection, is consequently depreciated.

Other terms, again without being given positive or negative values, find a divergent interpretation within the different systems, according to their main tenet. *Praty-ā-hāra,* lit. the grasping together and interconnecting forwards and backwards (*praty-ā*) means in the ontological system of the Vedānta : the folding-together of the world and its final dissolution; in the Yoga sense it is interpreted as psychologico-physiological concentration. *Praty-akṣatā,* lit. the reflection towards or backwards into the human eye, is for the realistic Nyāya the terminological designation of empirical perception, while the Vedānta, which finds its foothold in the concept of an extra-mundane Absolute, interprets *praty-akṣatā* as : reflection of the divine image. Both systems value *praty-akṣatā* in a positive sense, but according to their starting-point and aim they explain it contradictarily : as empirical or transcendental.

In accord with Indian feeling for natural counter-movements, though more strange for Western understanding, one and the same term may gain opposite meanings even in one and the same school. I recall the significance of *pra-saṅga* in positive or negative sense in the Nyāya texts. *Pra-saṅga* designates here either : the correct sequence or the wrong association. (Cf. also *Yoga-sūtras*, 3, 16, where logical discussions influenced by the Nyāya methods are introduced.) The Naiyāyika term *ā-kṣepa*, allusion and refutation, has a slightly different significance; here the meaning is not definitely opposite, but either neutral or negative.

Yet another problem which arises from the very nature of any technical term has to be pointed out. Besides those variable and elastic terms which are applied subjectively in the various systems, there are some, it is true, which are simply logical instruments of discussion in general. These, though they originated from the special needs and aims of the Nyāya, are later on used as neutral elements without any specific adaptation to the contents of the other systems, but are considered solely as formal instruments for every scholarly argumentation.

Before I undertake the main task of investigating the position of the various prefixes in the different philosophical systems, some more preliminary questions have to be raised. A remarkable fact, to be observed in no other language to the same degree and strength of expression, is the accumulation of two, or even more, prefixes in a single Sanskrit term. Do these different prefixes corroborate or contradict or merely modify each other? And are the rules of the relation between the different prefixes definitely fixed? In the course of studying the terms applied in the different philosophical schools one has to take account of this additional problem and to summarize the conclusions at which one arrives.

A further question arises as to the relation between the prefixes and the nouns or verbs to which they are added. Is it actually the case that all verbal roots, or their derivatives the nouns, require to be further stressed by a prefix? It is true that some of them are in themselves sufficiently pregnant with meaning and dynamic power so that there is no need for adding prefixes of direction. For instance, the metaphor of a cosmic dance, so often applied in the Sāṁkhya to explain the continuous transmutation and evolving motion of the *prakṛti*, is sufficiently expressed in the simple noun *nartakī*, the female dancer. And similarly the Nyāya applies the term *mānam* with or without the addition of prefixes to emphasize that the human reason is capable of measuring everything according to its own superimposed laws. I deal, in an appendix to this study on prefixes, with the problem whether the prefix or the noun is the essential bearer of meaning.

In exposition I venture to use two different though correlative methods. In the first chapters I outline the systems in hand as a kind of propaedeutic prelude, analysing the terms with prefixes so as to demonstrate that they are the very keywords of the various doctrines. In the further course of investigation, however, when expounding the systems of Sāṁkhya, Nyāya, Grammar, etc. I change the method intentionally in order to provide a counter-test. If it is really true, as claimed here, that the prefix-terms are the very exponents of the systems, then it should also be possible to work without, so to speak, this auxiliary scaffold of a preliminary summary of the systems concerned. I shall therefore occasionally start directly with the analysis of the very terms as themselves the representatives of the various systems. In these chapters it is left to the reader to combine the single threads, the various prefix-terms, to a systematic network.

2

The Single Systems and their Keywords

1. Vedānta[1]

The system which is most developed in all its consequences is probably the Vedānta. Nevertheless, its main tenet can be brought under a short formula. An immanent and transcendent unity, a super-personal Being as *Summum* is assumed; and this *Brahman* exists before, behind, within, and after, all empirical phenomena. From this postulate arises the fundamental Vedāntic problem : what kind of relation is to be supposed to exist between this assumed transcendental unity and the observable empirical plurality?

The choice of prefixes to be used for Vedāntic terms is made with respect to this basic Vedāntic problem. The prefix *adhi*, from above, is accordingly favoured. All actual facts are valued from the transcendental angle, from above. Terms like *adhi-ṣṭhāna* are accepted as a proper expression of the dependency of all worldly things on a superimposed order which is, at the same time, the basis and the ruling law from

1. Methodically the Vedānta system holds a singular position. One has to keep in mind that the systematic Vedānta is meant or at any rate pretends to be only a commentary on the concepts (and thus terms) of the Upaniṣads, the texts of Revelation. (cf. Śaṅkara, in his *Commentary on Vedānta-Sūtras*, 2, 1, 11 and elsewhere). It is thus not only admissible but necessary to insert in this system, but only in this one, pre-systematic (i.e. Upaniṣadic) terms.

above. If, on the other hand, not the transcendental but the human reason superimposes attributes and properties to the objects, then terms formed with the prefix *adhi* are applied which involve a deprecatory meaning. As such *adhy-ā-ropa* means : an erroneous application or superimposition. In the same way *adhy-asya* indicates : a false supposition (*Kā. Up.*, 5, 11, Comm.).

Other prefixes, too, are introduced in accordance with the general Vedāntic tenet. Polar notions are the natural outcome of the Vedāntic dogma. There is first the assumed polarity between the transcendental Constant and the empirical Transient. On the other hand, there is another kind of polarity to be observeed within the sphere of phenomena only. All actual objects are seen as continuously moving between the empirical polar stages of growth and decay and vice versa in the course of their reincarnation. The prefix which implies in itself this polar notion of counter-direction is *prati*. It finds accordingly a most frequent use in Vedāntic terms. *Prati-ṣṭhāna* (lit. German : the "Gegenstand" or "Wider-wurf", in the sense of the medieval German mystic) is the supporting counter-pole of all empirical beings. *Prat(y)-īka*, the counterpart, is the symbol of transcendental reality. *Praty-akṣatā,* the counterpart of all perceptible things, is the vision of the Divine, the reflection of the Absolute. It is, so to speak, as the literal translation suggests, a counterbalance of empirical perception. From outside (above) comes the *prati-bimba* or *prati-bhā*, the reflection of transcendental light.

Brahman has unfolded the world out of itself and reabsorbs finally all its emanations. It takes back all shapes into its infinite reservoir. This cosmic final function is termed *praty-ā-hāra*.

Praty-ag-ātman, the *Ātman* bent (*añc*) into the empirical sphere, is the individual soul, the empirical counterpart of the universal cosmic *Ātman*.

Terms provided with the prefix *ava*, downwards, are in congruence with the Vedāntic view that this lower world is governed from above by a constant transcendental power. *Ava-tāra* is therefore the term for the descending of the supreme power by the assumption of a personal shape.

The aim of Vedāntic metaphysics is to transgress the limits of this transient world of empirical frame and empirical perception. *Ati-tarati*, to transgress, and *at*(*y*)*-īndriya*, that what lies beyond our sense organs, is therefore the goal. *Ati*, the transcendental prefix, is another favourite for creating terms of Vedāntic metaphysical tendencies.

There is one aim given for all mundane beings : approach to the Divine. In the older Upaniṣads it is sought for with magical means. *Pra-viś* (*Bṛh. Up.*, 4, 4, 10), *upa-cāra*, *up*(*a*)*-āsanā*, and *upa-*(*ni*)*ṣad* is the going, or sitting, towards, i.e. the seeking contact and participation with the Absolute. This is not fully separated from the ordinary being[2] and therefore is approachable, while immanent though hidden. It is an aim which stimulates our longings and directs and lifts our tendencies. Therefore we urge forwards, *upa*. But once more, if we do not tend towards this transcendental goal but follow only our human reason and make our reasoning the master and driving force for its own logical aims, we are misguided; hence *up*(*a*)*-ā-dhi*, the rational and intentional (*upa*) attribution (*dhi*) is considered as misleading (cf. also the above-mentioned *adhy-ā-ropa*).

Quasi-mechanically and receptively we have to follow the inner urge towards getting a hold on the Transcendental . Here is the right place for applying the prefix *ā*. *Ā-lambana*, *ā-*

2. It is, however, occasionally also termed *ud-āsīna*, sitting outside, which is actually inconsistent with the Vedānta view, but consistent with the Sāṁkhya concept of the *Puruṣa* (cf. S.K. 20).

yatana, *ā-śraya*, all these are terms for seeking an ontological support and refuge in the constant *Brahman*.

Epistemologically, too, the Vedānta recommends receptivity. We cannot ask for more than to receive the *ā-bhāsa*, the reflection of the supra-mundane illumination. Our irrational urge (*ā*) will make us a suitable receptacle of higher powers.

And once more we have to view the polar side. All that which is a good tendency when directed towards the Transcendental, becomes wrong when satisfied with a merely empirical aim. Accordingly, prefixes designating the forward urge are apt to be used under certain conditions in terms of depreciation also. *Abhi-māna*, will- and thinking-power, simply directed towards worldly aims, is to be discarded as human *hybris*, overbearing.

The appreciation of transcendental as above empirical values, however, does not imply that the Vedānta is so world-remote as to deny the accidental importance of the empirical for its own limited sphere. *Vi*, the prefix indicating spatial dispersion, is applied in terms of spatial extension. *Vi-varta*s, the manifold emanations, are acknowledged as actual realities, but regarded transcendentally as illusions, because contradicting supra-mundane unity. On the other hand, even the *Brahman* may be combined with a term of a *vi*-compound; *vi-bhu*, being all and everywhere (*vi*), is an appropriate attribute of the *Summum*, when viewed from its empirical side as an all-embracing, ever-present and all-pervading power.

As I pointed out before, the Transcendental itself is viewed from polar aspects, and yet considered as a whole : it is not only transcendental and external, but at the same time also immanent and internal. As the latter it enters the empirical sphere and is united with every individual *Ātman*. This basic idea of unity clearly predestines the position which the prefix *sam* holds in Vedāntic concepts. The assumed primary union between the empirical objects and their transcendental place of support[3] is in the everyday life of the average man overshadowed by a secondary union, namely by physical or psychological attachment to worldly matters.

Here, too, the prefix *sam* finds its place, but it is used merely in a kind of neutral sense, while simply stating an empirical connection : *abhi-saṁ-pad* (*śarīram*), coming into contact (with the body) : *Bṛh. Up.*, 4, 3, 8, and *Tait. Up.*, 1, 1, 7; *saṁ-ni-pāta*, connection with empirical matter (*Bṛh. Up.*, 4, 3, 7, Comm.); *saṁ-sarga* (*pāpmanā*), association (with the material evil) : *Bṛh. Up.*, 4, 3, 8; *saṁ-baddha* (*karmabhiḥ*), tied together (with the *karmas*) : *Bṛh. Up.*, 4, 3, 22, Comm. — *Saṁ-sāra* designates the *sāra*, the wandering about of the *karma*-bearer through all kinds and shades of reincarnation. Here the prefix *sam* is added to indicate the wide range of possibilities which lie side by side in this series of rebirths (the usual translation, "cycle of rebirth," I ventured to repudiate for other reasons in my *Indian and Western Philosophy*, p. 16 f.).

The transition from the material attachment to spiritual union is illustrated by the simile of the partly physical, partly super-physical union of love. *Saṁ-pari-ṣvakta* (*Bṛh. Up.*, 4, 3, 21) is a significant term which depicts the complete embrace (*pari*); the meaning of the encircling function of *pari* is here enhanced and completed by the addition of the prefix *sam*.

---

3. It is not accidental that we find just in the Vedānta so many synonyms expressing the concept of support. These are terms in which the different prefixes are characteristically applied to indicate different stage of nearness and of dependence between the empirical individual and the transcendental whole. Either they denote the motion of approach (cf. the above-mentioned *ā-yatana*, *ā-lambana*, and *up*(*a*)-*ā-śraya*), or they illustrate that support is already reached, so that one can lean against it (*prati-ṣṭhā*), or that one can finally rest upon it being fixed and melted down (*ni-layana*) into a unity with the primary basis.

The final aim of regaining or rather recognizing the fundamental unity with the Transcendental is once and again expressed by Vedāntic terms formed with the prefix *sam*. The tendency towards this aim is very often emphasized by adding to the prefix *sam* yet another prefix which illustrates the forward, and at the same time a higher, motion. *Upa-saṁ-krama* (*Tait. Up.*, 2, 8) and *upa-saṁ-padya* (*Chānd. Up.*, 8, 3, 4), both designate the tendency towards (*upa*) *saṁ-krama* or *saṁ-pad*, the reaching of the union.

Similarly *abhi-saṁ-pad* and *abhi-saṁ-bhū* (*Chānd. Up.*, 8, 15, and 8, 13) denote intentional approach towards this last aim. *Saṁ-pra-sāda* and *saṁ-pra-mukta* (*Chānd. Up.*, 8, 4, 4, and *Bṛh. Up.*, 4, 3, 36) designate other attempts (*pra*) to come to a final enlightenment and thus deliverance by union (*sam*) with the Transcendental.

Pra-svapiti (*Bṛh. Up.*, 4, 3, 9) indicates a similar process of striving after this union. But this is only a temporary liberation reached in the state of deep sleep (*suṣupti*) which anticipates final liberation.

Before, however, this positive forward motion can set in, negative efforts must be mobilized in order to remove the veils or covers which have from outside overshadowed the clarity of the consciousness of this union. Here is the place for compounds formed with the prefixes *apa*, *vi*, and *nir*. *Apa-hata-pāpma* (*Bṛh. Up.*, 4, 3, 21, Comm.) means to beat off the evil; *vi-jahāti* expresses the same meaning, but according to the function of the prefix *vi* in a more extensive and intensive way : to discharge it. *Vi-pāpa*, *vi-rajas*, *vi-cikitsā*, to free oneself from evil, passion, and doubt (*Bṛh. Up.*, 4, 4, 23), and *vi-jara*, *vi-mṛtyu*, and *vi-śoka* (*Chānd. Up.*, 8, 1, 5) represent the emotional meaning of *vi* : to get rid of morbidity, death, and grief. Here is implied not only a statement of dispersion expressed by the prefix *vi*, but the intention of attaining such a dispersion. *Vi* designates here a dynamical process of carrying out the necessary purification instead of the mere assertion of no more evil, etc. Therefore the prefix *vi* is appropriately used instead of the plainly logical negation contained in the prefix *a*. The meaning of the prefix *vi* comes here near to the significance of the prefix *nir*, which is to be found in terms like *abhi-niṣ-padyate* (*Chānd. Up.*, 8, 3, 4) : after having destroyed (*nir*) the covers of obstruction, he comes forth.

The getting beyond these impediments is designated by the prefix *ati* (cf. above, p. 16). The term *ati-tarati* and *at*(*y*)-*īta*, to cross beyond, represents the continuous call for non-acquiescence in the empirical world.

Before attaining the static final union (*sam*), the reaching out from the lower empirical sphere upwards into the higher transcendental range must take place. *Ut-krama*, stepping outside and upwards (*ut*) is recommended in *Bṛh. Up.*, 4, 3, 8, as the last stride before attaining the extra-mundane Transcendental.

But as pointed out, the *Ātman-Brahman* is not only considered as a transcendental, but also as an immanent reality. Therefore, the very process of union with the Transcendental can also be reached by an inward motion. Concentration on the innermost part of the heart, as the seat of the microcosmic *Ātman-Brahman*, has to be achieved. Settling down into the subtlety of the pericardium is yet another way of perfection. Here is the adequate place for prefixes like *ava* and *ni*. Not the descent of the external Transcendental downwards into the empirical sphere, but the descent from the external Empirical into the immanent Transcendental is here visualized. *Anv-ava-krama* (*Bṛh. Up.*, 4, 4, 1) means to descend into the depth of the heart; *ny-eti* and *ni-gacchati* (*Bṛh. Up.*, 4, 3, 36) designate to go down into this subtlety (*aṇiman*) after having drawn together all vital forces from the extremities of the limbs.[4]

A few words may be added to illustrate also in this context the special significance of the prefix *prati*, which by its specific inclusion of opposite tendencies plays an important part in Vedāntic thought. The Vedānta is, as it were, always moving on two levels simultaneously, on the empirical and the transcendental. About *prati*, denoting forward motion from the external Transcendental into the empirical *Ātman*, I have spoken above. Here, in the exposition of the immanent *Ātman* the Vedāntic terms formed with *prati*, tending to the opposite direction from the individual *Ātman* into the Transcendental have to be considered. To reach the final aim of regaining primary clarity and union with the Transcendental the empirical bondage has to be shaken off, the evils have to be driven back : *prati-vah* (*Chānd. Up.*, 8, 3, 2). On the other hand, the door of communication between the individual and the transcendental *Ātman* must be reopended. This is expressed in *Kā. Up.*, 2, 13, and its commentary : *praty-ap(a)-ā-vr̥ta*. The accumulation of three prefixes suggests that a complicated process is here illustrated. The obstacles and covers (*vr̥*) have to be removed (*apa*), after the tendency towards the aim has

4. Here is an interesting problem: the occurrence of apparently Yogic ideas in the later Upaniṣads. The historical aspect of attempting to trace influences of the Yoga on the Vedānta seems to overlook the inner reasons which lie in the Vedānta itself. It is true that the external transcendental aspect of the Vedānta contains no possible analogies or similarities between both systems. The Vedāntic concept, however, of an immanent *Ātman* results in similar ideas to those of the Yoga. But yet there is a fundamental difference. The Vedāntic aim is given a priori; only the external impediments have to be removed. The Yogic goal, on the other hand, is to be achieved a posteriori, and to be attained, not to be regained, by appropriate exercises and training.

set in (*ā*) and the necessary reverse motion of reopening the access is expressed in *prati*.

Then finally, in the last stage of deliverance the prefix *sam* appears in a quasi-static meaning of union. The liberated one can rest in his concord with the Eternal. He enjoys the union with *Brahman* (*sam-aśnute*) : *Bṛh. Up.*, 4, 4, 7.

From the characteristically Vedāntic standpoint of viewing all things from the angles of both realities, the transcendental and empirical, from transcendental and empirical associations as final and primary conditions, and transitory stages between these two ends, we come to realize that a law of ever-present antinomies is operating in Vedāntic thought. This inner principle finds its formal and aesthetic reflection in Vedānta texts. The Vedānta is inclined to present its problems in the form of striking juxtapositions of opposites. An aesthetic viewpoint can accordingly also be taken in the special case of the Vedānta, but is less justified for the other Hindu systems. Rhetorical antithesis is an artistic means for mirroring dogmatic antithesis. Three, or even more, kinds of these parallelisms of strongly contrasted words may be found in the Vedānta. The same verb (or noun) is repeated with contradictory prefixes, or synonymous verbs are applied, which are once more varied by means of opposing prefixes. Or different verbs are introduced but are assimilated to each other by rhyme or alliteration not by any logical association. The contrast within all these parallelisms is introduced by the various prefixes applied. They alone give the distinguishing shades among the nearly related or identical verbs, which represent, as it were, the constant factors. *Anu-paśya*, look along to the former (in the series of reincarnations or emigrations) and *prati-paśya*, look in the opposite direction to the following — this is the emphatic teaching of *Kā. Up.*, 1, 6. The same artistic method, though not expressed by genuine prepositions, can be observed in the juxtaposition of terms like *āpta-kāma* and *a-kāma* (*Bṛh. Up.*, 4, 3, 21). Here, too, attention is drawn to the meaning of variation or different stages of development, by changing the first part of the compound, while the second part remains the same and thus throws into full relief the dynamic meaning of the prefixes.

Besides the prefixes *anu* and *prati*, which are contrasted merely as operating in opposite directions, terms with the contradictory prefixes *sam* and *vi* are frequently found in striking juxtaposition. In one and the same sentence supra-empirical union (*sam*) and empirical dissection into pluralities (*vi*) are brought face-to-face. *Saṁ-jñāna* (or *saṁ-y-ak-jñāna*), the fundamentally given all-consciousness, is constrasted with *vi-jñāna* : detailed, i.e. empirical, cognition.

Sometimes the processes of union with and renunciation of empirical life is depicted in detailed similes in which *sam* and *vi* are contrasted with each other; the renouncing of immanent unity for the sake of empirical manifoldness is later followed by a second renunciation, that of this plurality for the sake of final reunion. After being born (*jāyamānaḥ*) and having taken up an empirical body (*abhi-saṁ-padyamānaḥ*) and thus coming to a contamination with the evils of the world (*pāpmabhiḥ saṁ-sṛjyate*) a contrary motion of dispersing the evils (*pāpmano vi-jahāti*) is put into force to dispel this empirical union for the sake of transcendental reunion. An inner uplift leads to the higher level in the moment of empirical death (*ut-krāman mriyamāṇaḥ*) : *Bṛh. Up.*, 4, 3, 8. Here, nouns, verbs and verbal suffixes of similar sound are piled together, and in this confusing consonance the prefixes added give the distinction and direction.

In other important passages of Vedāntic dogma similar artistic means are used to enhance the significance of the teaching : as a falcon, after having flown about in all directions (*vi-pari-patya*), clasps his wings (*saṁ-hatya*) and melts (*saṁ-laya*) into the elemental simplicity of his place of rest, in the same way the *Ātman* turns home after the distraction and strain of empirical life and comes finally to his natural inner support (*Bṛh. Up.*, 4, 3, 19).

The Vedānta is on the whole not a dramatic but, as it were, an epic system. Though a kind of development takes place and a certain tendency prevails, it nevertheless never moves outside the range of its pre-established harmony : unity between the individual and the highest *Ātman* is always extant, though not always consciously realized. In so far, the Vedānta is in a way a static system, unlike the Yoga which dramatically acts and incessantly strives to reach perfection as a final but not immanent tendency of human will-power.

Epic similes of organic and inorganic life, sun and moon, ocean and river, root and bud, birds and goats, etc. are appropriate images in the Vedānta for corresponding biological processes in the human sphere. The seemingly external and artistic means of Vedāntic diction turns out to be deeply rooted in and determined by essential Vedāntic dogmas.[5]

Dealing with the Vedānta, not only with the early texts but also with the later systematics of its commentaries (especially Śaṅkara), a few remarks should be added on the general logical way of argumentation which each system has developed in its own defence and for the refutation of other systematic schools. Here we come across terms which are not the special property of the Vedānta, but are common instruments of logical disputation. We may select a few of these general logical terms. To enhance the dynamic meaning of the logical process they are mostly formed with prefixes

5. With the Vedāntic view of metaphors, abbreviated similes, I deal in another context later on p. 101.

designating either a forward motion or a fixation : *pra-vr̥tti*, function; *anu-bhava*, apprehension : *adhi-gama, upa-patti*, and *upa-labdhi*, grasping and understanding; *upa-cāratas*, metaphorically or allusively; *pary-āya*, synonym; *par(y)-īkṣaṇa*, complete investigation; *ni-rodha*, obstruction; *ni-yama*, logical rule; *an-ava-sthā*, ad infinitum; *prati-nyāyam*, corresponding to deduction, etc. These terms, however, have to be treated in greater detail at their appropriate place, i.e. in the Nyāya, where I shall point out the subtle significance of the prefixes applied.

But a few words must be added about terms in general. In this Introduction and previously in my essay "Deutung und Bedeutung indischer Terminologie", I pointed out that Indian terms are not Latin "termini" (fixed limits and unchangeable borderlines). Neither the simple terms nor the compound-terms with prepositions prefixed are definitely fixed. Some examples of Vedāntic terminology may be provided for this statement. *Up(a)-āsanā*, like *upa-ni-ṣad*, has, it is true, a specific terminological significance in the Vedānta. Nevertheless, even in this system it occurs in a sense other than that of true veneration and approach to the Absolute. In *Br̥h. Up.*, 4, 4, 10, it is significantly used as designating approach also to the *avidyā*, the empirical ignorance. Similarly, *vi-sarga*, a cosmogonic term for world-creation, lit. emission, is in *Chānd. Up.*, 6, 14, 1, applied in its plain biological sense of pouring out inner secretion. *Vi-mukti*, denoting in its metaphysical sense deliverance, means in *Tait. Up.*, 3, 10 (2), a low physical function, the emission from the anus.

Simple terms, and still more compounds charged, so to speak, with the currents of prefixes, are centres of forces which work in many directions and do not operate through one channel, e.g. rational fixation only.

2. Mīmāṁsā

Mīmāṁsā is a theoretical doctrine (the name suggests the repeated reflection, *man*), but is concerned with practical religious aims and rites. Transcendentalism and Realism are more intermixed in Mīmāṁsaka theory and religious practice than in any other system (see a kind of intermixture also in the Nyāya programme proclaimed in *Nyāya-sūtras*, 1, 1). While Nyāya is both in means and in immediate ends concerned with realistic problems, which only in their last consequence are sublimated to establish a transcendental perfection (Liberation), Mīmāṁsā already in its primary ends, though not in its means, reveals super-realistic tendencies.

The Mīmāṁsakas are realistic Transcendentalists. Believing in *śabda*, the Holy Word, and *artha*, the essence of things, they try to make these religious and super-empirical canons of truth conform with the general pattern of *praty-akṣam* (realistic method). They empiricize, as it were, unempirical objects to make them more convincing for the *laukika*, the ordinary mind. The materialization of subtle matter (Religion) is here attempted for pedagogical reasons.

On the other hand, the Mīmāṁsakas are Dynamists, Functionalists. Action in itself counts, not the agent (cf. *Mīmāṁsā-sūtra*s, 1, 5, and Comm.). The latter's existence may be inferred from his actions, but the function alone matters and is the actual proof. Here we may discover definite remnants of primitive practical magic.

It is in the light of the strange combination of Transcendentalism, Realism, and Dynamism, taught in the programmatic introduction (loc. cit., 1, 5) that we should interpret the main doctrine of the Mīmāṁsakas and their keywords. Accordingly, certain prefixes are preferred. There is a prevalence of *vi* and *ut*, both belonging to the sphere of empirical notion, but partly applied in super-empirical axioms.

Strange to the Western thinker is the fundamental Mīmāṁsaka concept of a dynamico-biological and at the same time eternal Transcendental (*nitya*).[6] The main tenet of the Mīmāṁsakas, unique even in Indian philosophy, is that *śabda*, the word, is *aut-pattika*, spontaneous, and as such it is connected a priori with its super-empirical essence (*artha*).[7] As to the term *aut-pattika* : the prefix *ut* suggests in itself an evolution or a spontaneous motion which, like fire, sends out sparks in all directions. The noun to which this prefix is added tends to the same meaning : *pad*, to go, or *pat*, to fall. Both combined suggest an action like a biological springing forth or budding out.[8]

It is characteristic that *śabda*, sound, is here taught as having the capacity of springing forth spontaneously into being, as it were, from nowhere, from the not differentiated *ākāśa*. As a lamp reveals immediately and simultaneously itself, its instrument (the wick) and the surrounding objects, *śabda* reveals in one function the verb, the sound, and their meaning. *Aut-pattika*, the immediate activity, is opposed by the Mīmāṁsakas to *kṛtaka*, empirically or artificially produced.[9]

The concept of *śabda* has in this system two aspects : first, the religio-transcendental one. *Śabda* means here Veda, the

6. Here one sees that the usual translation of *nitya* as immutable-eternal is not always adequate.

7. The term *artha* is used in this system in its ambiguous meaning of either being eternal essence or rational application (see about this more in detail my *Sphoṭa and Artha*, Poona Oriental Series, No. 75, pp. 221ff.)

8. We may compare this concept with the Vedāntic simile of *śuṅgā ut-patitā*, the bursting out of the sheath of a young bud (*Chānd.Up.*, 6,8,3). The root *pad* (see above) comes under the influence of the prefix added near to the meaning of the root *pat*.

9. In *Mimāṁsā-sūtras* 1, 2, 3, ff., *uc-cāraṇa*, the purely emotive utterance, is opposed to rational international designation (*abhi-dhā-na*).

revealed eternal truth. In accordance with the aim of Mīmāṁsā, which is the exegesis of the Veda, Vedic authority is fully alive and never effaced as a merely external but binding tradition, as is the case in some parts of the other so-called "orthodox" systems. Secondly, and secondarily, there develops out of this religious belief a profane aspect, the study of psychological linguistics and phonetics. Each single word, its intonation and sounds, is holy and significant, and because divine Vāc is the medium of revealing Vedic truth, every profane word and sound indirectly participates in its transcendental power. At this point Vedic exegesis and the first stages of philology are still connected with magic.

From yet another angle there is a second seemingly empirical science based on transcendental axioms. No other philosophical Hindu system has developed such subtle subdivisions of the canons of cognition, *pramāṇas*. But it is not logical refinement which underlies the fact that the Mīmāṁsakas established, in addition to the four recognized *pramāṇas*, the fifth and most intricate one, that of *arth*(*a*)-*ā*-*patti*. This should not be translated abstractly as "inference from circumstances by implication", but literally and with regard to the dynamic meaning of the prefix and noun applied. The prefix *ā* combined with the noun *patti* designates the moving (*pad*) towards (*ā*) the *artha*. Undisturbed then by the accidental non-perception of an object on one place, its presence on another place must be inferred, because its existence is known as certain according to its *artha*. The *artha*, the pre-empirical and empirical reality of things or facts, is a cardinal dogma of the Mīmāṁsakas, transcendental Realists as they are. The *arth* (*a*)-*ā*-*patti* proof can be usefully contrasted with the apparently similar theory of the *a-bhāva* in the Nyāya to reveal the basic differences between the primarily empirical Naiyāyikas and the fundamentally super-empirical

Mīmāṁsakas. The positive-psychological Nyāya theory is concerned with the act of perceiving, not with its object; it does not seek, so to speak, the object in another place but is satisfied to state its non-existence at the expected spot and to value the non-perception itself as a positive mental act.

Vi, the prefix designating singleness and diversity, is applied for the chief term of ritual ceremonies and their explanations in the Mīmāṁsā: *vi-dhi*. The pointing out of all and every possibility of subtle variations and slight differences expressed by the prefix *vi*, may appear merely practical and pedantic. But here, too, practical means and actual diversity are but the symbol of super-empirical ends. Ancient ritual belongs to the sphere of magic which at the same time is practical and supervisible (*a-dr̥ṣṭa*) in its effects. Each minute variation in the performance of a rite produces a far-reaching macrocosmic result. Actual cause is magnified in its effects. Therefore, *vi-dhi*, every single religious performance, is scrupulously to be taken into consideration, and every *vi-dhi*, differentiation, has to be accounted for. Similarly, this explains the meaning of *vi-kr̥ti*, the various derivations of *karman*, the main sacrifice.

The same ambiguity between Transcendentalism and Realism prevails in another Mīmāṁsaka term formed with the prefix *vi*, though with a slightly different tinge. *Vy-añjana*, the manifestation (from *vi* and *añj*, curved apart) or *abhi-vy-añjana* is contrasted and combined with the *aut-pattika* stage of words. Though the *śabda* exists a priori, before its first empirical shaping into sounds, it does not get its practical significance till its *vy-añjana* or *vy-akti* is performed. *Vy-añjana*, or *abhi-vy-añjana*, the quasi-mechanical emanation of the word and its *artha*, is a kind of translation into the empirical sphere. As in the *prakr̥ti* of the Sāṁkhya, all *vy-akta*s, all emanations, are already potentially pre-existent in the stage of *sat-kārya*, the *śabda*s of the Mīmāṁsā are potentially existent before their actual realization in the moment of their first utterance.

3. Sāṁkhya

Let us now turn to the transcendental-empirical system of the Sāṁkhya. Besides the usual explanation of a transcendental Dualism between the principles of Matter and Spirit, the so-called Sāṁkhya "Dualism" can be interpreted also in other ways. First, there is the Dualism between two constant Absolutes (*prakṛti* and *puruṣa*), which are transcendental. On the other hand, there is also an empirical Dualism between their evolutes (*puruṣa*s and the emanations of *prakṛti*).[10] These concepts then in their activities belong to two spheres, the transcendental and empirical. A duality is therefore necessarily expressed in the corresponding terms and prefixes. *Vi-veka*, separation of Matter and Spirit, is the primary state and the final aim, while *vi-kāra*, change of form, *vi-varta*, illusionary change or modification, *vi-śeṣa* and *vy-akta*, in the empirical sphere, means dispersion, i.e. a multiplicity of the evolved phenomena. But yet a third significance of the prefix *vi* arises in certain Sāṁkhya terms which are the common property of logical argumentation. *Vi* is used as designating logical dispersion in the sense of not being fixed. *Vi-pratyaya* means a confused concept, i.e. one which is not *ekāntika*, not conclusive (lit. not one-sided). *Vi-paryaya* is similarly : an erroneous view. Taken, on the other hand, from the realistic angle, *vi* means in *vi-kalpita* : the discriminate things, things as they are given in their actual empirical diversity. Another meaning of the prefix *vi* is common to Sāṁkhya psychology and similar investigations in other systems : *vi-śoka* and *vi-rāga* mean freeing oneself (*vi*) from sorrow and passion.

10. However, not all schools of the Sāṁkhya take into consideration the empirical reality of a plurality of *puruṣa*s.

Also other prefixes come into the foreground, if we are concerned merely with the empirical range of evolution and transmutation of manifested *prakṛti* : *pari-ṇāma* indicates transmutation of Matter, like the revolving clay on the potter's wheel, and represents a term of significant dynamics and continuity (*pari*), encircling, but intermittent capacity (cf. *Yoga-sūtras*, 2, 20, Comm.).

There is an immanent though perhaps unconscious tendency in the course of emanation of the manifested *prakṛti*. *Prakṛti* itself designates the urge of production; *kṛti* must be taken here in both an active and a passive sense, producing and produced. It is as much action as function. It is not the agent that matters but the result. Therefore the Sāṁkhya speaks of eight *prakṛti*s, the eight upper stages of manifestation, of which only the first has the sole capacity of merely producing, while the following seven have the ambiguity of being both agent and product. We may grasp this double function in the emanating process under the simile of the Cabbalah (Zohar, 1, 19b and 20a). What is a receptacle when seen from above, becomes the cover of the next below, which is going to be unfolded. The whole process of emanation is a kind of progress. *Pra-pañca* is the unfolding of original Matter into the manifoldness of individual forms. While in the Neo-platonic concept of emanation every lower emanation is considered as a degradation, the Indian concept seems mainly to be a biological concept of evolution; it contains primarily a mere statement of a process, irrespective of ethical canons of value. The prefix *pra* indicates a natural process (urge). *Prakṛti* is called *pra-sava-dharmin*, in the sense of having the immanent quality of productivity. Even the last and final stage of emanation which inverts into its opposite (re-absorption), is nothing but a quasi-mechanical course of development. *Pra-laya* is a melting process (*laya*); it turns back in a circular motion to its starting-point. In a way this process implies a teleological view, but it serves its purpose unconsciously as milk is produced within the cow at the appropriate time for feeding the calf : *pra-vṛtti* (cf. *Sāṁkhya Kār.*, 57). As to the specific quality of the *guṇas*, the prefix *pra* plays also its part; here *pra-vṛtti* is called the emotional urge of *rajas* (passion), which is counterbalanced by *ni-yama*, suppression, the quality of *tamas* (inertia). Yet another aspect of the prefix *pra* is revealed by the term *pra-kāśa*. This is the immanent quality of *sattvam*, the *guṇa* of static balance, and as such means : continuously shining forth without a special urge.

A different shade of meaning of the prefix *pra* seems to be implied in yet another, though perhaps later,[11] Sāṁkhya term. *Pra-dhāna* is a synonym for *prakṛti*. *Prakṛti*, however, is here not viewed from its biological aspect but, as the term *dhāna* suggests, belongs here to the sphere of logical reasoning and measuring. Accordingly, the prefix *pra* is here used in the sense of "superior" or "prior". *Pra-dhāna* is a designation of *prakṛti* as the foremost principle (cf. for this meaning the discussions on *pra-dhāna-karma*, in *Yoga-sūtras*, 2, 23, Comm.). As the *puruṣa*, her spiritual counterpart, is called *adhi-ṣṭhāna*, superintendent, *prakṛti* is here provided with a title of rank not of function.

A limited value in this system is allotted to the prefix *sam*. Here the empirical phenomena are not viewed as lying side by side on a same level in extension (*sam*), but are manifested successively. Accordingly, the all-embracing character of Matter is expressed by no synonym formed with *sam*. *Sam* implies generally a centripetal function, which is later on compressed, while *prakṛti* is regarded as having the capacity of a primary centrifugal motion (*vi*). In the sphere of the Absolute there is also no room given for the meaning of the

---

11. Cf. E.H. Johnston, *Early Sāṁkhya*, p. 26, and elsewhere.

prefix *sam* as a static connection between the two transcendental principles, *prakṛti* and *puruṣa*. In their pure super-empirical meaning they are conceived as fundamentally opposed to each other. Only in their momentary empirical co-operation there is a place for terms like *saṁ-yoga*, union between *prakṛti* and *puruṣa*. Even when viewed from the angle of the *prakṛti* and her emanations only, there is no proper use for the application of the prefix *sam*. Instead of by *sam*, the not yet dispersed and not yet functioning equipoised *prakṛti* is designated by the prefix *a* (logical negation). Thus, *prakṛti* is also called *a-vy-aktam*, the pre- or not yet manifested Principle. The transcendental state of unity before manifestation is here conceived from the posterior empirical state; the prior is but a postulate and therefore only negatively termed as something not yet unfolded, not yet (*a*)-*vy-aktam*. Unity is nothing else but not yet diversity (*vi*).

Sam is therefore applied only in terms which are not characteristically Sāṁkhya, but generally logical or psychological. *Sam-ud-aya*, it is true, is used to denote the co-operation (*sam*) of the three *guṇas* in producing the various phenomena, but in this co-operation they are not co-equals; one dominates, while the other two are overweighted. Otherwise the Sāṁkhya speaks of *saṁ-moha*, complete confusion and *saṁ-kalpa*, imagination, *saṁ-jña*, naming faculty or *saṁ* (*s*)-*kāra*, complex of predispositions or latency of former impressions but all these terms formed with *sam* are the common property of several systems.

The same holds good for the two transcendental prefixes *parā* (*paras*) and *ati*. Because the Sāṁkhya is fundamentally realistic and can only investigate the empirical stages of *prakṛti* (and the *puruṣas*), nothing but negative attributes drawn from the positive Empirical are applied to the postulate of the transcendental Principles. These are merely assumed as necessary *ā-śrayas*, basic material matters like a canvas for painting (*S.K.*, 41). Accordingly, *parokṣa* (from *paraḥ-akṣa*) is only a loanword in the Sāṁkhya. In the same manner the Sāṁkhya borrows the word *at(y)-īndriya*, i.e. what lies beyond the range of empirical perception.[12]

A few words may be added on those terms which are applied in the different systems in a similar sense but, in accord with their main tenets of investigation are interpreted either from an ontological, psychological, or transcendental angle. *Up(a)-ā-dāna*, literally : acquisition or grasping, means in the psychological sense of the Yoga, grasping the organs of sense and withdrawing them from the external world, drawing them, so to speak, towards the inner Self; in Buddhism, on the other hand, this term of grasping is applied exactly for the reverse process of grasping the empirical matter for the sake of a new incarnation. In the Sāṁkhya, however, this grasping is viewed from the transcendental aspect; *prakṛti*, the material cause, is grasped as a fundamental support.

Other terms which play no special part in the Sāṁkhya but are merely used in the generally accepted way, may be omitted from this short survey : *abhi-māna*, arbitrary self-pride; *saṁ-ghāta*, aggregate; *adhy-ava-sāya*, ascertainment; *apa-varga*, liberation (opposite to *bandha*, bondage); *vy-āpti*, universal pervasion, i.e. correct implication, etc.

---

12. *Āti-vāhika*, a designation for the *sūkṣma-śarīra*, the subtle body, is according to A.B. Keith, Sāṁkhya system (The Heritage of India Series, 2nd ed., 1924, p. 110), a late Sāṁkhya concept. Here, it is true, a transcendental prefix (*ati*) is applied, because a kind of transcendental notion is assumed. But this is not a genuine concept of eternity. The subtle psychological aggregates persist only for a certain time (from one incarnation to another) but not *ad infinitum*. They transgress one empirical existence only to return to another one and, besides, at a certain time this whole process of transmigration comes to a final end.

The Sāṁkhya, the enumerative system (*saṁ-khyā*), provides less opportunity for dynamic counter-processes, and accordingly does not use a wide range of dynamic prefixes as most of the other systems do. As its very name suggests, the prefix *sam* is here preferably used in its static sense of lying side by side, i.e. classification. The only dynamic process which is here demonstrated is that of dispersion and emanation. As such the prefix *vi*, together with the prefix *pra*, holds a key position in the Sāṁkhya.

4. Yoga

A psychological supplement to Sāṁkhya ontology is provided by the Yoga system. The general opinion that the Yoga has furnished the atheistic Sāṁkhya with a theistic basis does not seem to hold good when one investigates more closely the *Yoga-sūtras* and *bhāṣyam*. *Yoga-sūtras*, 1, 15 Comm., and 3, 26 Comm., give a significant explanation of *aiśvaryam*. This term definitely refers here to the capacity of psychological mastery, freedom from impediment, attained by the Yogin himself. Mostly it does not refer to any theistic belief in the interference of a God from without. Yoga stands for self-activity and self-liberation. The Yogic dogma does not take its starting-point from the two transcendental principles *prakṛti* and *puruṣa* like the Sāṁkhya. Scientific systematics, objective statements, or enumerations (*saṁ-khyā*) of divisions and subdivisions are not essential for the Yogic aim, which is purely practical. This distinction between Sāṁkhya and Yoga is clearly hinted at in *Bhagavad-Gītā*, 3, 3, where after the theoretical explanation (Sāṁkhya) the practical application (Yoga) is introduced. In accord with the practical tendency of Yogic efforts the term *pra-sāda* has the physico-psychological meaning of clearing and purifying the gross matter of the body by adequate exercises rather than the implication of a concept of divine Grace of enlightenment. Perfection of the Yogin is reached by physico-psychological self-development. Self-activity and intentional effort is the basic prescription in Yogic teaching and practice.

The prefixes in Yogic terms are chosen accordingly. *Pra* and *abhi* are decisive means of expression for showing the way forward towards perfection. *Pra-bodha,* lit. the striving towards (*pra*) enlightenment (*bodha*) is thus the appropriate term. *Pr*(*a*)-*ānta*-(*bhūmi*) is the stage marked by longing towards the last state (*pr*(*a*)-*ānta*) of self-liberation. *Pra-yukta,* one of the most frequent terms, means to be intent, concentrated (*yukta*), on the way towards development in yoga. To grasp the objects which serve this purpose, to eliminate those which hinder it, is expressed by *pra-yukta* and *a-pra-yukta*.

The prefix *anu,* though also indicating a kind of forward but also regressive tendency, does not play an essential part in Yogic concepts. *Anu* designates, as pointed out in reference to other systems, a movement which follows another one which is already formerly laid down. Therefore this prefix is not in accordance with the Yogic fundamental tendency of ascending by stages on ever-changing, ever higher levels.

To throw oneself towards a new aim is pregnantly expressed in the Yogic term *abhy-āsā* which is, in general, too vaguely translated as "exercise" and "training", the strong dynamic aiming not being indicated thereby. *Abhi-gama,* going towards, approaching, is another synonym for the Yogic conscious forward tendency. *Abhi-ni-veśa* indicates through its two prefixes two tendencies combined : the striving forwards (*abhi*) and the fixing down (*ni*). As pointed out in the exposition of the Vedānta, every effort directed to the desired aim is useful, but the same display of energy in a reversed direction produces just as much harm. Brāhmaṇas and ancient Upaniṣads warn us once and again that wrong sacrifice is worse than no sacrifice. Accordingly, one needs to beware of *abhi-ni-veśa*, poured-out energy (*abhi*) secured and concentrated by an additional downward motion (*ni*) which strives after and settles down on objects of sensual pleasure, such as are detrimental to Yogic liberation. Dynamic forces expressed by the prefixes are effective, but gain a positive or negative meaning according to their respective aims. *Abhi-māna*, pride in the efforts of human reasoning and pre-mature fixation, also lies outside the way of Yogic perfection. The Yogin prepares himself to become a cosmic receptacle and can never be satisfied with human reason, which is based on the fiction of an isolated consciousness, and thus hinders cosmic union.

The prefix *adhi* indicates forward tendency and its result, a kind of progress to a higher view. *Adhi-ṣṭhāna* (cf. *Yoga-sūtras*, 3, 49) has to be viewed with reference to the criticism set out above of the Yogic concept of divine Grace. The Yogin, too, is conscious of needing a *sthāna*, a place of support; but provides it himself by reaching a higher hold through his own effort. Like a mountaineer, he himself gains his places of rest and security, he prepares the footholds to which he draws himself higher. These successive footholds, steps hewn by the climber's axe, are adequately termed: *bhūmis*, Yogic stepping-grounds.

Vi-tarka, the dispersing force (*vi*) of decomposing reasoning (*tarka*), is rejected by the Yogin who strives after concentration. *Vai-śāradya*, on the other hand, is welcome as a dispersing function of removing all stains which hinder spiritual clarity (cf. *Yoga-sūtras*, 1, 10 Comm., and 1, 47).

It may well be that the study of the immanent meaning implied in the prefixes used in the Yogic keywords results in a psychological test for the successive development from one Yogic stage to the following ones. The prefixes applied for the terms of the successive *bhūmi*s display in their specific tendencies a consistent development of Yogic training.[13]

At first the preliminary task of the yoking-together (*yoga*) of bodily and mental powers has to be fulfilled. Accordingly, the prefixes suggesting forward tendency are applied for this first stage of uplift. The forces have to be led straight to the point in the desired direction. *Abhi* and *pra*, and in some way *adhi*, are here the appropriate representatives. But the Yogic path is exhausting and slippery; once and again the Yogic texts contain the warning against relapse which might cause the mind to lose the ground which has just been gained. Therefore the result must be secured, must be fixed. Terms with the prefix *ni*, holding down, have in this second stage[14] their proper place *ni-yama, ni-rodha, ni-yoga*, and *ni-vr̥tti*, do now occur, or with a similar significance *ava*, like *ni*, is used (cf. *ava-sthā*).

As to the prefix *ni*: it must decidedly be kept apart from the prefix *nir*. While *ni* suggests merely a fixation or stopping of a flow in the sense of stabilization, *nir*, on the other hand, implies annihilation by splitting up, i.e. the complete atomization of the thing expressed in its accompanying noun or verb. *Ni-vr̥tti* is a restraining of the *vr̥tti*, function; *nir-vr̥ti*, which is often wrongly translated in the sense of *ni-vr̥tti*, however, designates a kind of explosive destruction of each

---

13. Actually there are given divergent subdivisions of Yogic stages in Yogic literature. My analysis does not agree with any of them technically, but tries to grasp the general trend underlying all of them: the law of Yogic developments starting with the dispersion of distraction (*vi*) tends to fixation (*ni*) and reaches by inverted movement (*prati*) final concentration (*sam*).

14. Already, at the begining of the upward tendency on the Yogic path, an adequate position is given to a term with the prefix *ni*. While *yama*, restraint, is prescribed for all bad tendencies, *ni-yama*, abiding in the good tendencies, is advocated. These shall in further progress on the Yogic path be developed.

linear motion and of fixation. It results in radiate motion and, being thus all-motion without any distinct direction, it has eventually the same effect as no tendency at all.[15]

Ni-vṛtti then, in the sense of the Yoga system, has a double aspect; fixation of the desired function and restraining, on the other hand, of the unwanted tendency.

And now to the third stage of psychological development of the Yogic *bhūmi*s. The intensity of direction of the first Yogic stage, accentuated by the prefixes *pra*, *abhi*, etc. being accumulated in the second stage[16] by stopping their outflow (*ni*), has now further to be completed by encirclement. Here the function of the prefix *pari* is required. *Pari-karma* means : accumulated, because embanked and confined, action. The next step is to lead the flow of forces into another channel, to draw it back into the inner centre of activity. From the outside direction, which is the natural ontological tendency, the vital power is now inverted and bound backwards to the psychological reservoir. *Pari-karma* is now transformed into *prati-karma*. Just as the tortoise draws within its shell its extended limbs for its own protection, so the Yogin withdraws his senses and their capacities[17] into his inner centre of force (*praty-ā-hāra*). Thus he gains his *prati-ṣṭambha* or *prati-ṣṭhāna*, resisting power and support. The prefix *prati* is the expression of such a redirected and thus accumulated activity and resisting force.

The prefix *prati*, in its ambiguity and manifold functions, reveals even more of its different aspects in the complicated

---

15. Cf. to this point the explanation of *śūnya* and *śūna* in my *Polarity of the Indefinite*, Coomaraswamy Jubilee Volume 1938, and my interpretation of *Nirvāṇa*, in Modern Review, Calcutta, 1939.

16. See note 14, p. 38.

17. Cf. also the term *ā-vṛtta-cakṣuh*, whose eyes are turned backwards (*ā*) in *Kā. Up.*, 4, 1, where Vedāntic and Yogic ideas converge (see the above remarks on Vedānta).

Yoga thinking. Counter-agents against undesired results of natural development are mobilized by Yogic power. *Prati-pra-sava*, counter-creation of the Yogin's consciousness, is the subjective-positive application, whilst *prati-kūlam*, lit. which runs against the flow (of tendency), represents a negative-subjective implication. *Prati- kāram*, counter-action, is set forth by the Yogin as a positive-subjective act; *prati-sarga*, on the other hand, is acknowledged in the sense of the Sāṁkhya *pra-laya* as an objective-ontological counter-movement by which all emanated Matter is reabsorbed. The quasi-mechanical reflecting power of *prati* is accepted even for the highest stage of Yogic perfection. *Praty-ava-marśa*, reflection, is for the Yogin not an action performed by his thinking and pondering mind, as it is for the Naiyāyika, but a kind of mechanical automatic influence directed towards him, the most perfect receptacle for higher vision. *Prati-saṁ-vedanā*,[18] on the other hand, is an active function which he deliberately performs as an inverted accumulation (*sam*) of consciousness, and as such it forms the positive counterpart to *praty-ā-hāra*, the merely negative withdrawal from the external world.

The specific Yogic *siddhi*, perfection, which results from the third as well as from the fourth stage is *antar-dhāna*, lit. the inward position, but usually translated as "faculty of disappearance from external visibility". Here, once more, the rendering generally adopted seems to efface the concrete meaning and to point only to the practical result. It thus fails to reveal the psychological process. Following the dynamic steps indicated by the prefixes used one may understand the significance of this Yogic *antar-dhāna*. Not only does the Yogin gain concentrated power for himself by directing forwards, settling, and redirecting inwards, his poured-out energy, but he can, in this highest stage of perfection, also interfere with

18. Cf. *Yoga-sūtras*, 1, 29 Comm. : *prati-saṁ-vedin*.

the natural perceptions of others. He cuts off the rays which render his body visible by his intense inner concentration, and thus intercepts also the passive capacity of being seen. According to India's specific theory of perception, the object of perception is more active in this process than the subject (cf. *Kā. Up.*, 3, 10, and *Bṛh. Up.*, 3, 2, 1 ff.). Thus, the Yogin as object has the faculty of making himself a no-more-object. While seeing, he is no more seen (one may venture to view from this angle also the Vedāntic concept of *Brahman-Ātman* with regard to the concept of "the unseen Seer").

In being concentrated in himself the Yogin comes to the perfect balance and harmony. Here is the place in the Yoga for the prefix *sam*. *Ni-yama*, the function of the preliminary stage, becomes now *saṁ-yama*, balance and complete (*sam*) restraint (*yama*). *Sam-ā-dhi* is the result of this effort, the composed mind, collection of all vital forces without distraction and diversion. *Sam* is opposed to *vi*, which presupposes and wants empirical divergencies. The Yogin, therefore, as soon as he has attained the position of *sam*, is no more attached to any single accident and incident. He is now their master; he has acquired *sam-ā-patti*, the all-attainment. Here in this highest Yogic stage, all the different shades of meaning implicit in the prefix *sam* come into full relief. *Sam* means here : ontological fullness, physico-psychological concentration, and ethical balance and composure.

The ontological fullness thus attained finds its expression in different forms. First, the perfect Yogin is *sarva-vit*, all-knowing, i.e. he possesses the *saṁ-pra-jña*, the all-embracing knowledge.[19] He is aware in a kind of simultaneous consciousness of all his former incarnations also and besides in a comprehensive way, of the forms of pre-existence of other beings.

19. Cf. similarly : *saṁ-prati-patti* (*Yoga-sūtras*, 3, 17 Comm.) and *prati-saṁ-vedin* (*Yoga-sūtras*, 1, 29 Comm.).

Psychologically, too, he has full self-control, and control of other phenomena around him. Though he is not capable of altering fundamentally the course of Nature — this would be against the foremost Hindu axiom of Nature's almightiness — he can influence the speed of her course. He may accelerate (*upa-krama*)[20] and he may reduce (*nir-upa-krama*)[20] the quickness of natural development. But whatever mastery the Yogin may attain through his accumulated power he never ventures to make himself or one of his human capacities, say reasoning, the self-sufficient factor.

Unlike the Naiyāyika, the Yogin keeps himself prepared, so to speak, as a receptive vessel for higher vision. Therefore, even at his highest stage of perfection, there is still room for terms formed with the prefix *ā*, the quasi-mechanical universal forward motion. *Ā-bhāsa*, receptive vision, reflection, mirroring something around or above him, is not beneath the Yogin's dignity. Truth comes towards him (*ā*) from outside. *Ā* is the prefix working in both directions, from the subject and into the subject.

A somewhat similar concept which has a further special significance of its own is that of *nir-bhāsa*. *Bhāsa*, the spiritual light which is diffused (*nir*) into small particles all over the world, can be grasped by the subtle capacity of the perfect Yogin, and even one of its rays suffices to bring him complete enlightenment. Prepared by the gradual stages of development the Yogin is now capable even of another way of highest visualization. *Yoga-sūtras*, 1, 47 Comm., state that *kramān anurodhī sphuṭaḥ pra-jñ(ā)-ā-lokaḥ*, the Yogin's vision of knowledge, can arise not (only) in complying with the stages step by step, but as a spontaneous act in a sudden flash of revelation or intuition.

20. Cf. *Yoga-sūtras*, 3, 22.

A most significant feature with regard to the problem treated is revealed in the Yoga system more clearly than in all the other philosiphical schools of India. The dynamic tendencies of the single prefixes in their intentional and also in their quasi-mechanical function are here thrown into full relief. Secondly, double or even multiple prefixes are in the Yoga preferably used to accentuate the motions and counter-motions; intensity and restriction, forward urge and fixation; both, forward and backward motion reflected or counteracted, etc. (cf. *vy-ut-thāna*,[21] *vi-ni-yoga*, *pra-ṇi-dhāna*,[22] *saṁ-ni-dhi*[23]). More about these multiple prefixes in a special chapter later on.

A third peculiarity of Yoga notions may be observed. The Yogin, even in this life, views all phenomena not only as intensely subjective, but also in the detached sense of objectivity. Things are seen in their polar relationship to each other : *vidyā* and *a-vidyā; darśana* and *a-darśana; liṅga* and *a-liṅga*, all these are *prati-dvandvins*, counterparts. Precisely because he strives to attain non-attachment towards the external world, the Yogin is driven to the epistemological acknowledgement of all the polar tendencies within the phenomenal world. He sees the *prati-dvandvins* as necessary correlations; they are *praty-ā-sanna*, inter-related and yet opposed one to another. They are natural opposites : *prati-pakṣas*. Thus, the Yogin reaches a complete knowledge (*praty-ava-marśa*[24]) by viewing everything in its polar aspect or relativities alike in the ontological, psychological, and ethical spheres.

---

21. *Vy-ut-thita* : *Yoga-sūtras*, 2, 1 Comm.
22. *Pra-ṇi-dhāna* : *Yoga-sūtras*, 1, 23; 2, 1; and elsewhere.
23. *Saṁ-ni-dhi* : *Yoga-sūtras*, 2, 17 Comm.
24. This term is variously to be interpreted according to the various stages of Yoga training.

5. Nyāya

In accordance with its general scope it is in the Nyāya system in which the greatest number of terms is to be found. For this fact an inner and an external reason can be proffered. Terms, "termini," are an outcome of the tendency for definition. It is no accident that in logical argumentation derivations of the root *mā*, to measure, are frequently used. Secondly, all other systems borrow Naiyāyika terms for their method of scholarly discussion as technical means because, according to its very programme, discussion in all its variations is the chief subject of the Nyāya.

The Nyāya, being primarily concerned with realistic facts and their logical explanations, and using discrimination and discernment, finds from the nature of its aims the fullest use for the prefix *vi*. *Vi-tarka*, decomposing reasoning, is the immediate aims and the means of Nyāya operations (cf. contra Yoga). Unlike the Vedānta, which tends to immanent and transcendental unity, Nyāya revels in the dissolving process which is implied in the most appreciated Naiyāyika function of *tarka*, crumbling into pieces, as this term onomatopoetically suggests, i.e. strict analysis of all empirical facts. *Vi-veka*, discernment, is an originally agricultural term indicating the sifting of a discrete single thing out of the undiscernible mass. *Vi-ṣaya*, the single object, shows the same prefix[25] and its inherent *vi-śeṣa*, distinction, lit. remaining apart, is the main object of Naiyāyika research. *Vy-ava-sthā*, decision, means lit. to single out something from the general basis. Similarly, *vy-ava-sāya*, determination, contains the idea of separation and

25. A derivation of this term from the root *viṣ* is philologically unlikely. From the point of view of psychological philology (a method specially favoured throughout this essay), if any term, then this calls for the prefix which indicates divergency, i.e. the prefix *vi*.

consequent fixation. *Vy-ā-pāra* is the practical proceeding (root *pṛ*), indicating dispersion (*vi*) and distribution (*ā*), an act of decomposing in order to handle single phenomena. Its synonym *vy-ava-hāra* reveals the same process. *Vi-bhu*, all-pervading, applied in the transcendental Vedānta for pointing out the empirical efficacy of the Absolute, is used in Nyāya Realism in a similar sense of *vy-āpti* : correct implication, general logical validity.

The prefix *vi*, in its dynamic function, serves for the terms of passionate logical refutation. *Vi-kṣipta* scatters the basis of the opponent's argument. To designate the resolution of turning over the whole ground of argumentation sometimes even a stronger prefix than *vi* is needed. Here *nir* has its place. *Nir-vacanīya*, that which can be explicitly said and tested, is that which has been wrought up to its finest subtleties. Similar is the concept of *nir-ṇaya*, conclusion, deduction, lit. the decomposing leading into all and every direction and thus reaching final knowledge. The very term reveals a significant difference between the Indian and Western syllogistic process (from *syn*, together). Not comprehensiveness and generalization, but thorough and discerning scrutiny is the Naiyāyika aim of deduction.

Besides representing the merely spatial dispersion the prefix *vi* gains sometimes a secondary purely logical meaning. *Vi-pratyaya*, *vi-paryaya*, designate the dissolving of formerly fixed determination. Here, the addition of *vi* turns the term into the negative, while taking away and uprooting established statements.

As pointed out for the Yoga, the prefixes *upa*, *pra*, etc. emphasize the forward direction and tendency. Logic, too, can use them for the purpose of grasping things (epistemologically). *Upa-labdhi*, *upa-patti*, both meaning : understanding by grasping or approaching, are based on the fundamental Optimism, Positivism, and Substantialism[26] of Hindu thought. The dynamic meaning of *upa*, approach, is here evident. When the result of the approach, the contact between object and sense organ, is to be emphasized, the prefix *sam* is further added : *sam-upa-patti*. Whatever I aim at, that I reach, and that inevitably I grasp, I understand and hold (cf. the magical Brāhmaṇa-texts which repeatedly display this belief). *Upa-cāra*, identification by resemblance, and *upa-naya*, application and conclusion, are the logical outcomes of this primitive concreteness and belief in the infallibility of functions. *Upa-māna*, analogy, lit. measuring one thing to — or upon — another, is once more a proof of this material outlook on logical grounds. No doubt is allowed with regard either to the first process of perception or to the second; the desired end can be reached. *Abhy-upa-gama*, to grasp and to accept, shows the same concrete and positive attitude. Besides intentional forward motion the prefix *upa* implies in logical consequence a certain limitation; what is gained in intensity, is lost in extension. Accordingly, for instance, *upa-lakṣaṇa* means synecdoche of a part for the whole. In a similar manner *upa-deśa* means instruction in the sense of specification.

Pra-saṅga, to stick towards something, means logical consequence. However, according to the context, it may assume also a negative meaning : wrong association (in this double sense it is used also in the other systems, when the instruments of logical argumentation are borrowed from the Nyāya; cf. e.g. *Yoga-sūtras*, 3, 57). *Pra-yojana*, motive, on the other hand, is a Nyāya term most probably adopted from the psychological Yoga.

Anu expresses the following of a way already known. *Anu-māna, anu-vy-ava-sāya*, secondary cognition, is literally : the

26. Cf. my exposition of the Indian theories of perception in *Indian and Western Philosophy*, p. 81. f.

measuring along or settling along an established perception; it indicates the intentional repetition of a former direction.

A slightly different shade of meaning is revealed in the term *ānv-īkṣikī*, the view along and survey of all things, a term used for philosophy as a generalizing science. But *anu* sometimes also suggests the reverse direction, the drawing towards oneself an object which existed independently without. *Anu-bhava, anu-bhūti* mean : becoming aware of a thing. Even the Nyāya, in spite of its main tenet of the dominant human mind, acknowledges in accord with the general Hindu theory of perception a receptive stage of the subject with regard to the object.

Ni, the prefix expressing fixation (cf. the above remarks on Yoga), plays certainly a prominent part in this system of definition. The name *ny-āya* itself contains the prefix *ni*. Nyāya means : settling down, fixation. *Ni-gamana*, conclusion, is a kind of synonym for Nyāya.

In a similar manner *ava* is used : *ava-dhāraṇā*, limitation, decision; *ava-bhinna*, splitting off, specification. *An-ava-sthā* is: *regressus in infinitum*, e.g. the not having settled down (*ava*).

Pari is connected with *ni* as in the Yoga system. *Pari-graha*, encircling and grasping; *pari-bhāṣā*, definition, evidence by circumscribing; *pari-cheda* (lit. to cut around) means : contouring, outlining, defining. *Pari-caya*, recognition, is lit. the compilation around; *pari-śeṣa*, completion, is : encircling the remaining thing. *Pari-codanā* means : strong (*pari*) stimulus rousing activity of thought (*codanā*). Again, the Naiyāyika aim of finality is not the ideal of an all-embracing comprehensiveness, but accurate fixation of limits and of complete exclusion of obstruction.

The prefix *ā* to express wide, quasi-mechanical direction, which is not governed by intentional purpose is also used in this system of logic, though not with preference and for the most part with a negative significance. *Ā-deśa* means : vague and general indication. *Ā-kāṅkṣā* designates : dependency. The *pramāṇa* of *arth(a)-ā-patti*, which plays an important part in the Mīmāṁsā (cf. above) is of only secondary importance in the Nyāya. *Ā-bhāsa*, in the term *(hetv-)ā-bhāsa*, is a fictitious reason. The dynamic sense of *ā*, in which human intent does not play a decisive role, is repugant to the logical Nyāya mind.

The prefix *prati* has a bi-polar significance, and only when used in its forward direction of conscious tendency or in its backward direction as a restraining and checking motion it appeals to Naiyāyika thinking. *Prat(y)-īti*, approach to the subject, means lit. contact and collision, i.e. understanding. *Prati-jñā* is : assumption in syllogism tending towards the knowledge which is going to be established. *Prati-saṁ-vedanā*[27] means : accurate knowledge, i.e. counter-proof; *prati-pra-sava*, counter-exception is lit. a counter-production.[28] *Prati-ṣedha* is refutation, prohibition as counter-action. In these last examples the prefix *prati* represents the fighting spirit of passionate logical disputation.

Besides, *prati* is used in the sense of a corresponding counter-part. *Praty-āmnāya*, a synonym for *ni-gamana*, means the counter-part of the assumption, i.e. conclusion. *Prati-yoga*, the counter-union, is the classical term for counter-part. *Praty-ā-satti* is analogy, setting a new thing against another already known. *Praty-abhi-jña*, recognition, is a kind of repeated acknowledgement, not unlike analogy. *Praty-ava-sthā* is accordingly counter-condition. The bi-polar manner of thought is a characteristic feature of all Indian discussions. Position requires counter-position.

---

27. Cf. also *Yoga-sūtras*, 1, 29. Comm.

28. Cf. also *Yoga-sūtras*, 2, 19. Comm.: *prati-sarga*.

When, however, *prati* occurs in the meaning of a mechanical backward motion, neither the favourable nor the neutral use is acceptable to the dominant Naiyāyika thinker. *Prati-bimba*, receptive reflection falling into the human mind, is a term of disparagement like *ā-bhāsa* (cf. above), very much in contrast to Yogic and Vedāntic thoughts.

Sam, the prefix expressing co-extension, acquires a special shade of meaning from the logical Naiyāyika outlook. *Saṁ-bandha* and *saṁ-yoga* mean : connection in the sense of association. *Sam-avāya* means mutual interconnection between two inseparably related things and as such inherence. *Saṁ-ni-dhi* is : sequence and interrelation of members of a sentence in juxtaposition; *saṁ-sarga* is natural association through co-production. *Saṁ-patti* is completion; *saṁ-kalpa* (opposite of *vi-kalpa*, alternative) means an emotional decision, not favourably viewed from the Naiyāyika standpoint.

Another inherent meaning of *sam*, that of combination, is logically interpreted as generalization. Thus, *saṁ-ketaka* is a general agreement, and *saṁ-prati-patti* is a generally accepted concept.

The prefix *pra* has not a strong intentional meaning and has in a way a middle position between the quasi-mechanical *ā* and the fully intentional prefixes *abhi* and *upa*. *Pra-kāśa* and *pra-siddhi*, for instance, mean : becoming evident. *Pra-vac* and *pra-brū*, used in the terms of logical commentaries, have a slightly different tinge. They designate the function of propounding and proclaiming the meaning of the text to be commented upon.

Significant for the tendency of a philosophical system are the prefixes which are preferably used, so also are those which are partly or wholly neglected or even rejected. From this angle we have to view the prefixes *parā* and *ati* in the Nyāya. Both designate a longing to transgress final borders.

Parā occurs in the term *par(ā)-ā-marśa*, contemplation, lit. the rubbing towards and beyond. It plays only a part with reference to the repeated thorough handling of a thing (*mṛś*).

The prefix *ati*, however, which, stronger than *parā*, influences the term to which it is added in the transcendental direction, is distinctly treated with suspicion by the Naiyāyika thinker. *At(y)-īndriya*, that beyond the senses, means something undefinable and therefore lying outside the range of logical fixation. *Ati-deśa* is : extended application, it is something which cannot be defined and counts as a logical error. *Ati-pra-saṅga* is: an unwarranted stretch of a rule; and *ati-vy-āpti* is something which suggests more than intended and more than can be safely included in a proposition.

But now comes a strange but characteristically Indian fact: even the Nyāya Realists, who proved themselves in all their researches as so deeply concerned with this world only and its given distinctions, proclaim in the very first *sūtra* of their classical textbook that all their empirical means and ends are only a preliminary stage leading up to the *Tattva-jñāna*, the essential knowledge, which is just a way, one way only, to the attainment of the irrational postulate of Liberation : *Niḥ-śreyasa.*

The Nyāya Realists are fundamentally religious Transcendentalists, just as much as all the other Hindu systems of Liberation. The Naiyāyika only views this and the "Other World" not simultaneously, but successively.

6. Vaiśeṣika

Vaiśeṣika terms may be treated as an appendix to the Naiyāyika terms, the Vaiśeṣika being on the whole simply a supplement to the realistic epistemology of the Nyāya in the domain of realistic physics.

Accordingly, terms formed with the prefix *vi* are the most characteristic in the Vaiśeṣika terminology, too. The very name Vaiśeṣika suggests that the research of this system is mostly concerned with the *vi-śeṣa*s, the differences of physical objects in actual existence. The objects are investigated, both in their relationship of accidental differentiation and from the aspect of their spatial co-ordination. As such the Vaiśeṣika is a realistic synthetic system approaching the standpoint of the pure Materialists, the Cārvākas, who investigate the mere contact and connection of given phenomena. Here the prefix *sam* has its proper place. The various compilations and aggregations of Matter or given facts are explained in the Vaiśeṣika. *Saṁ-yoga*, connection, and *saṁ-ghāta*, compilation, are assumed to build up the physical objects. *Saṁ-śleṣa*, a merely external unpenetrating connection, as between the wood and the varnish, is a subject of Vaiśeṣika investigation.

Sam, as well as *vi*, its counterpart, is here dealt with from the view of physical extension, diversion, and connection.

All these actual conditions are, however, mere accidentals. Thus, even when the prefix *pra* is applied, it is not taken in its intentional but simply in its quasi-mechanical function. *Pra-caya*, loose accumulation, means that amorphous porous Matter is heaped into one mass. *Praśastapāda* speaks of *eka-pr̥thaktva, dvi-pr̥thaktva*, etc., that is to say, all objects represent a numerical addition of one or more separate single forms. In the main the Vaiśeṣika is concerned with static single entities which have only a loose external relationship. Even when the Vaiśeṣika speaks of *ā-dhāra-bhāva*, which Faddegon, *The Vaiśeṣika System*, p. 412, translates as "streamlike process", a static concept underlies the Vaiśeṣika view. Its meaning is merely a construction, or reconstruction, of aggregates.

In the pursuit of this fundamental study of the differences (*vi-śeṣa*s) of physical objects (*vi-ṣaya*s) it is true that later

Vaiśeṣika tries to find a systematic unifying, though not a unique, principle of explanation. The Vaiśeṣikas become then the *Kaṇādas* or *Kaṇa-bhakṣas* or *Kaṇa-bhakṣaṇas*, i.e. the "atom-eaters" or "atom-crackers".[29]

The fundamental Vaiśeṣika dogma of singleness or of mere compilation of Matter without, as it were, a transmitting electric current, is never given up, even when basic principles are postulated as primary entities or *dhātus*, primary elements of all things. The characteristic discovery, or rather final deduction, of the Vaiśeṣika is the dogma of atoms, of *aṇus*. Given facts of separate singleness are systematized and, so to speak, eternalized. But once more the Vaiśeṣika here, too, is reluctant to give up the safe ground of visibility. Only a compilation of multiple atoms is considered capable of providing a conceivable empirical reality. Even when such fundamental simpleness as a primary atom is assumed, the analytical decomposing tendency which is a genuine counterpart of compilation, does not stop short at this. The problem arises, whether even these assumed fundamental entities, these primary elements, the atoms, may not be further decomposed by the separation of their parts. Thus, a new kind of materialistic problem is raised : cannot the intensity of these atoms be reduced to a mere question of volume and quantity? Even when the Vaiśeṣikas reach beyond the sphere of observable experience, their method of empirical research and of its problems is till retained. It is true that in the investigation of atoms the non-empirical and apparently transcendental term of the *a-dṛṣṭam* (invisible) is introduced. But this principle of *a-dṛṣṭam* in the Vaiśeṣika terminology does not seem to have any theistic or ethical implications, as in the other systems, e.g. Mīmāṁsā. It only indicates the presence

29. On this subject cf. my "Zur indischen Namenskunde", *Geiger-Festschsrift*, p.139.

of an empirical entity beyond the sphere of empirical visibility which can be deduced from its visible combinations (cf. Faddegon, loc. cit., p. 221).

This very deduction, which has its starting-point in empirical facts, seems, it is true, to give rise to a kind of new metaphysics. The Vaiśeṣikas have established in a way a theory of relativity. All empirical things, as simple observation proves, have but an accidental and relative size. The infinitely small, the atom, and the infinitely great, the *ākāśa*, the ether, are however assumed to have a static and, as such, an absolute extension, either as the immeasurably smallest or the immeasurably greatest. Here, the Vaiśeṣika touches on the problem of the polarity of the Indefinite underlying *śūnya* and *śūna*.[30] But it is an esential feature of the Vaiśeṣika that these problems are not an outcome of transcendental tendencies, but the ultimate consequence of empirical observation.

Furthermore, the prevailing tendency of all Vaiśeṣika thoughts is not a transcendental dynamics like emanation, etc. but rather a kind of static construction. It is strange to observe that the very stress the Vaiśeṣika puts on objective physical observation and the statement of given facts dims, in a way, its correct view of actual dynamics.

After these preliminary remarks let us now turn to the prefixes applied in Vaiśeṣika terminology. The character of the system predestines the limited range of the prefixes to be used.

The prefix *vi* is accordingly in true Vaiśeṣika terms not viewed from the dynamic angle as an outflow from a former unity, but generally as statically asserting different facts which are already given.

The Vaiśeṣikas, it is true, accept a category of motion which bears the significant name of *karma* in its plain primary sense

30. Cf. my *Polarity of the Indefinite*, p. 91 f.

of activity without any tinge of ethical or metaphysical implication, as in the other systems. It is subdivided into the different physical functions of *ut-kṣepaṇam*, throwing upwards; *ava-kṣepaṇam*, throwing downwards; *ā-kuñcanam*, contraction; *pra-saraṇam*, expansion, and *gamanam*, going. Here a stage of function is expressed by prefixes or pregnant simple nouns differing from that found in most of the other philosophical systems. The prefixes are represented in the Vaiśeṣika in their primary simple meaning, not as figurative or psychological tendencies, but as plain physical spatial motions, and as such we may regard these Vaiśeṣika prefixes as an instructive counter-test to the investigation of the philologico-philosophical functions dealt with in this essay. It is noteworthy that in the true Vaiśeṣika terms multiple counteracting or corroborating prefixes are hardly ever applied. Simple physical motions, not complicated counter-movements, are investigated in the Vaiśeṣika. Whenever more complicated compounds of prefixes are to be found in the Vaiśeṣika, it can generally be inferred that Nyāya or Mīmāṁsā terms are adopted. Vaiśeṣika researches in the psychological theory of perception or of logical processes of discussion are taken from the Nyāya; psychologico-metaphysical dogmas of Vedic *śabda*s, sounds and words, are borrowed from the Mīmāṁsā. These latter adaptations justify the Vaiśeṣika claim to belong to the "orthodox" systems, pervaded, as it is, by traditional theories. But even here the specific Vaiśeṣika trend of thought sometimes transforms the loanwords into its own way of thinking. *Saṁ-ni-dhi* illustrates in Vaiśeṣika terminology nothing but spatial accidental proximity. *Pari-māṇam*, measurability in the sense of definite *quantity*, is accepted as a given fact for all single objects which can be circumscribed (*pari*), but gains the significance of an eternal *quality* in the two assumed Vaiśeṣika principles of quantity, whether in the minute atom or in the infinite *ākāśa*. Measure as infinite quality is a characteristic freature of Vaiśeṣika's quantitative thinking.

To conclude, the Vaiśeṣikas are the most consistent realistic thinkers. They are not psychologists (cf. contra Faddegon, loc. cit., p. 14); they are not metaphysicians; they are not concerned with ethical problems (cf. Vaiśeṣika *karma*-theory); but they are physicists and realists going so far in these deductions that they assume supra-visible consequences which can — or could — not be tested.[31]

It is not accidental that hardly any other philosophical system of India contains so many pregnant similes of everyday life as the Vaiśeṣika. The activities of a goldsmith, a blacksmith, or a varnishing worker are illustrations and, at the same time, starting-points for Vaiśeṣika investigations.[32]

Empirical facts are classified as individual entities. Prefixes and simple terms are applied in their concrete primary meaning. *Dvandva*-compounds, aggregative compounds, are used with characteristic frequency. Later on we shall note in the Jaina system a somewhat similar attitude towards realism and towards the problem in hand, the prefixes of their keywords.

7. Terminology of Grammar

A few words may be added on the terminology of grammar; for grammar, though not one of the six orthodox systems of

---

31. But again, even the realistic Vaiśeṣikas, like the Naiyāyikas, do not stop at physics as the final aim and end in itself. The Vaiśeṣikas, too, postulate as the final goal of all their empirical studies, to reach the *niḥ-śreyasa*, the *Summum Bonum*, of Liberation. Realists they are, but through way of Realism they long for, as all Indian schools (with the only exception of the strict Lokāyatas, the World-addicts), for a final religious Salvation.

32. The use of similes taken from everyday life are favoured in the Vedānta for reverse reasons (see in chapter "Vedānta", in *The Technical Terms of Philosophy and Poetry* and in "Epilogue").

philosophy, is in India nevertheless a recognized philosophical discipline. Pāṇini, past-master of linguistic science, is considered in true Indian manner as a philosopher and as a religious saint. The latter appellation derives from the pre-classical concept of the divine Vāc, to which I referred in the section on the Mīmāṁsā.

The linguist is in a way an initiated priest. Besides, the grammarian is a systematic thinker, bent on analytical research and on the adequate classification of his results in precise terms.

Most of the specific terms of Pāṇini, however, do not fall under the scope of this special study. They are not genuine terms, but artificial abbreviations for mnemonic purposes, and have to be explained in full by oral discussion. As I ventured to suggest in "Zur Psychologie der indischen Grammatik" (*Archiv Orientální*, 1935, p. 71) a general law and solution of Pāṇini's terms may be found in the fact that the first representative (*a-c*), or the last (*ha-ḷ*), or the most frequent (*ti-ṇ*) is taken for the designation of its whole group. A "dumb" consonant is added to indicate that no single example but the whole class to which it belongs is meant. The terms of Pāṇini are accordingly not terms but a kind of code-words.

Of the real terms to be found in grammar, some are common to grammatical science and to the occasional linguistic digressions of the orthodox philosophical systems. Grammar being an analytical science is significantly termed by a compound formed with the prefix *vi*. *Vy-ā-karaṇa* and its synonym *vi-graha* express pregnantly the tendency of grammatical thought. The nearly synonymous term *nir-ukta* (etymology) goes further in the decomposing process. According to the meaning of the prefix *nir* it does not stop at analysing the parts of a sentence but lays bare the verbal roots. Owing to the fundamental belief that word and sound have a quasi-biological function, Indian grammar is not satisfied with a merely decomposing activity. Words have, as explained above in dealing with the Mīmāṁsaka theory of *aut-pattika*, both a spontaneous urge and continuous life. The complex of sounds creates without intermedium its corresponding sense. The life-force of one sound penetrates its neighbour. Thus, we find more developed in Sanskrit than in any other language phonetic assimilation in regressive and progressive order. *Pra-saraṇa*, the change of a semi-vowel into a vowel or vice versa means : transformation by influence. *Pra-yoga* and *pra-yojana*, application of a word, mean not only a static logical but a dynamic functional expression. *Pra-vṛtti*, abstractly translated as "sense of a word", may be visualized under the simile of the stretching forward of tentacles.

Vi-pari-ṇāma, a term well known in its meaning of evolution or modification of the Sāṁkhya Prakṛti, gains in grammar a logico-grammatical but nevertheless a fully dynamic meaning. It suggests a change of case or suffix for the better understanding of a sentence (cf. *Mīmāṁsā-ślokavārttikā*, 1, 55).

Praty-ā-hāra, which I explained in its Yogic and Vedāntic sense as final reabsorption of emanated Matter into the *Brahman*, or as a contraction of psychological forces, has an equally dynamic meaning in linguistics: it indicates that several letters or suffixes are subsumed under a single syllable. A keyword is formed through contracting a whole series into one word by combining the initial letter of the first with the final of the last. *Praty-ā-hāra* means here: condensation.

The prefix *sam* occurs in grammatical terms in its extensive meaning. *Saṁ-jñā*, designation, is a proper name which is generally acknowledged. *Sam-ā-khyā*, assertion, is an assumption corroborated by the agreement of all; *saṁ-prati-patti* (cf. e.g. *Yoga-sūtras*, 3, 17) is a concept of general validity.

Vi-bhakti, inflection of noun, case-termination, means

literally: partition. The stem of the root radiates in divergent directions in consequence of the local dynamics of the case.

According to its analytic method grammar frequently concurs with Naiyāyika thought. *Ati-vy-āpti* and *ati-pra-saṅga*, where *ati*, the prefix transgressing all borders, is applied, gains thus a negative sense. The fullness suggested by *sam* is an accepted concordance, while the almost unruly character of *ati* ventures to jump over the boundaries of grammatical rules, and thus is used pejoratively.

A slightly different shade has in grammatical terms the second transcendental prefix, *parā* (*paras*). *Parokṣa* (*paraḥ-akṣa*), that which lies beyond the senses (eyes) and is, as such, a significant term for transcendental, means in grammar simply "past tense", i.e. that which cannot be witnessed by the speaker. As *Yoga-sūtras*, 3, 13, and Comm., expressly teach, there is no natural connection possible with the past. Indian dynamics always tend to future stages of development. The past is dead for India's realistic manner of thought (one of the reasons why India shows, on the whole, no interest in history). *Parokṣa*, then, as a grammatical term (past tense) acquires in a way a pejorative implication, in striking contrast to its lofty significance in the Hindu metaphysical system of Vedānta.

8. General Terms of Hindu Philosophy

In the course of the exposition of the Nyāya some species of general terms had to be dealt with. These are general logical terms which are accepted by the other systems as a logical instrument for scholarly discussion. Other terms, too, are the common property of all systems, because they express aims and ends common to them all. Either they reveal the objective aims of philosophy in general or they hint at empirical or esoteric subjective ends common to them all. A significant example of the first group has been given before. *Ānv-īkṣikī* reveals in its very name, through the dynamics of noun and prefix, the aim of Hindu philosophizing. *Ānv-īkṣikī* is literally translated: the look along and survey of all things. The empirical facts and their inter-connections are reviewed (hence, the application of the prefix *anu*) in a kind of bird's eye vision; philosophy is valued as the generalizing science.

Common to all systems, too, are some religious and social ideas and, accordingly, their keywords. *Saṁ-sāra* is the interconnected (*sam*) wandering (*sar*) through all different shapes of incorporation.

The generally acknowledged social concept of Hinduism is the dogma of the *ā-śrama*s, the different stages of life. The various physico-psychological and intellectual needs of childhood, manhood and old age are taken into full consideration; the Hindu assigns to the receptive stage of youth the duty of learning (*brahmacārin*); to the fully developed physical needs of manhood, the duties of a married householder (*gr̥ha-stha*) and of practical work; and to the time when physical forces decay and the development of spiritual wisdom is reached he assigns the *ā-śrama* of the *vāna-pra-stha*, the duty of giving up community-life and taking refuge (*pra*) in the forest for undisturbed teaching and meditation. The sublimation and perfection of this third stage is reached by the *saṁ-ny-āsin* in the fourth stage of complete (*sam*) renunciation, lit. the casting off or throwing down of the world and its attachments. Thus, every stage of life obtains its adequate time of fulfilment, and accordingly acquires its specific peace of mind. *Ā-śrama* is in noun and prefix an appropriate term for this, designating literally: coming to rest.

Eschatologically, too, there is one concept common to all divergent schools of Hindu thinkers. Their final aim which, in a way, already rules even their empirical tendencies, is to get rid of all limitations. *Apa-varga*, lit.: the pushing away (*apa*) of *varga* (enclosure), is the term for seeking and finding Liberation, salvation. The Infinite is conceived as that which remains when all finite shapes, when all portions of Time and Space, when all measures, when all numbers, are removed.

Some further general terms are perhaps even more characteristic for the problem under consideration, because they are formed from one and the same root, which gets its different meanings by contrasting prefixes. Thus, *ni-gama* and *ā-gama* are precise terms through the very tendency inherent in *ni* and *ā* respectively. *Ā* is the prefix of extension, functioning, so to speak, on the horizontal line, while *ni*, downwards, indicates a vertical movement, which as soon as it reaches the horizontal line results in fixation. Accordingly, *ni-gama* designates the Vedic truth from above, or anything which is finally fixed, and *ā-gama* a continuous sequence of tradition, a proceeding line of succession.

9. Buddhism

A few remarks on the terminology of the non-orthodox philosophical systems, Buddhism and Jainism,[33] may be added in conclusion. The difficulty of representing Buddhist keywords with regard to the significance of prefixes lies in the fact that Buddhism is not only a system of thought, but combines the aims of a mass-religion, of a developed psychology and aspects of mere logic and epistemology all in one. Accordingly, the prefixes in question have here an embarrassing wide range in their possibilities. They have to be viewed together with the terms to which they are added in three different contexts: in the empirical, in the logico-epistemological, and in the psychologico-eschatological spheres.

Frequent Buddhist sayings, attributed to Buddha himself,

33. Buddhist and Jaina terms will be given in Sanskrit, not in Pāli and Prākrit.

state that the first aim of Buddhism is the explanation and valuation, or rather the devaluation, of this world. Afterwards the development of logical and psychological capacities has to set in, in order to enable us to escape from the wordly entanglement. As such, significant Buddhist terms are firstly applied for the closer examination of the empirical data. These researches make use of ontological facts and conditions, discriminate them with logical means, and later psychological reflections arise, but only then when the super-empirical goals have been recognized. The characteristic fact, however, is that Buddhism only ventures to give a lead up to the borderline between the Empirical and the Transcendental. It hardly ever dares to give a closer description and any definite statement of that which follows (or precedes) empirical existence. Whenever Buddhism speaks of the Transcendental, it draws a sharp distinction between the "Beyond" and the Empirical. It views these two worlds as a pair of opposites, as *laukika* and *lokottara*, as *saṁvṛti* and *paramārtha.*

Thus, one cannot expect in Buddhism, as in the Vedānta system, terms with the prefix *ati* in its metaphysical import.[34] A continuous transition from the Empirical to the Transcendental, expressed by a term with a prefix, by a compound, is not adequate to the Buddhist fundamental view that both worlds have to be kept apart. Accordingly, the bird's eye-view from above, expressed by a compound with the prefix *ava* seems not to be taken either from the metaphysical aspect,[35] except perhaps in the late concept of *Ava-lokita-īśvara*, the

34. The prefix *ati* appears only in its general sense of "extremely" or in the pejorative sense of "too much". As such it occurs in terms like *aty-aya*, as transgression, i.e. sin, or in logical discussions as transgression of a possible definition. I pointed out this latter sense in the treatment of the Nyāya system.

35. Again, the prefix *ava* is also applicable in the logical sphere; *Ava-bhāsa* means: hint. Here in a way is also taken a view from →

Bodhisattva who out of compassion, looks indiscriminately (*ava*) downward on the less advanced souls in order to draw them nearer to his higher, though not yet final, stage. This example represents, however, more a kind of theistic-personal than an impersonal-transcendental outlook on the Highest, as is the case in the Vedānta.

With regard to the terms belonging to the first stage of empirical investigation, the Buddhist sees the phenomena in their ever-changing dynamic processes and their fullness of co-ordination. Accordingly, the forward tendency of longing for material existence in general and some single objects in particular finds its expression in terms formed with the prefixes. *Abhi-ni-veśa* is: the addiction to empirical objects. *Abhi-māna* is : the desire and intent.[36]

Ā-srava is the influence of and receptibility for empirical objects and conditions. *Ā-yatana*, *ā-laya*, and *ā-dhāra*[37] mean seeking a hold (on actual data). *Up(a)-ā-dāna* is : taking up the

→ above, i.e. from the higher standpoint of the expert. *Ava-sthā* and similar terms express logically: to find a support in valid, i.e. already proved, conditions. *Ava-vāda* means : instruction given by the expert; *ava* is used here in the sense of the German "unter-weisen". It is a significant fact that the Buddhist terms formed with the prefix *ava* are often intermixed in the process of translating and re-translating from Sanskrit into Pāli, and vice versa with terms containing the prefix *apa* (*ava-* or *apa-dāna*; *ava-* or *apa-lokita-īśvara*). This seems to prove that in Buddhism the view from above (*ava*) is not strongly felt.

36. From the higher aspect of renunciation, however, all these empirical attachments are later depreciated, and thus it may sometimes appear as if the prefix *abhi* implies in itself a pejorative sense. Not the prefix *abhi* but its application in terms of empirical tendencies brings in this effect. Thus *abhimāna* gains the meaning of "wrong imagination"; *abhi-saṁ-plava* similarly becomes then "confusion".

37. Cf. its use with Dharmakīrti (O. Strauss, *Indische Philosophie*, München, 1925, p. 217).

conditions of empirical existence and appropriation of worldly objects. *Anu-śaya* is: clinging towards a new reincarnation by restoring the activities of the *kleśa*s, i.e. following (*anu*) foundations given.

The prefix *prati*, too, is applicable in the empirical sphere as designating the actual opposition of empirical tendencies and counter-tendencies. *Prat(y)-ītya-sam-ut-pāda* is the mutual interchaining (*prat(y)-ītya*) of links of empirical existence.

When regarding the phenomena in their co-ordination, the prefix *sam* is applied in its meaning of spatial collection. *Saṁ-(s)kāra* is: the combination of the various conditions for a (latter or former) empirical existence. *Saṁ-ghāta* is: the compilation of aggregated elements for further embodiment. *San-tāna* is: the combination of *kṣaṇa*s, moments of existence. *Saṁ-sparśa* is: the spatial contact between a sense organ and its object. Saṁkhyā is in this context : empirical consciousness;[38] *saṁ-jñā* is: empirical awareness.[38]

The empirical divergency is indicated by terms formed with the prefix *vi* in its meaning of diversity; for instance, *vi-kalpa* is: diffused (*vi*) imagination.

After having completely acknowledged and explained the phenomena of this world in their embarrassing fullness of facts and conditions, in their diversity and confusion, the logical tendency of selection and discrimination sets in. Here, however, Buddhism does not invent many new terms which are not to be found in similar significance in Hindu logic also. *Pra-vṛtti* is: logical process; *pra-sādhana* is: logical solution. *Upa-yoga* is: logical application; *Upa-darśana* is: indication. *Upa-saṁ-hāra* is: intentional (*upa*) summarizing. *Abhy-upa-gama* is: hypothetical (subjective) proposition. *Adhi-pati*[39] expresses

38. For other meanings see later on in this Chapter.

39. For other meanings see later on in this Chapter.

logical dependency. *Adhy-ātman* means (as in the Vedānta): concerning, with view on, the *Ātman*. *Ūha-apa-ūha* is: thesis and counter-thesis. *Vy-añjaka* is: insinuating a meaning.

Far more characteristic, the most characteristic I venture to say, are those Buddhist terms which occur at the turning-point from the psychological to the eschatological sphere. After having grasped and devalued the empirical phenomena, a new tendency of finding a hold in something which leads beyond them sets in. *Saṁ-vega*, the complete (*sam*) perturbation, is the uprooting of formerly acknowledged foundations, and as such the first step to conversion.[40]

Being thus freed from the clinging towards the lower empirical sphere new supports are now sought. *Ni-śraya* indicates: support given by the practical means of strict regulation; *ni-yama* is: the self-imposed religious observance and results, psychologically, in ascertainment and determination towards the aim of Buddhahood. *Ava-bodha*, becoming fully enlightened from above, a term applied for the enlightenment of Buddha and the perfect Buddhist saints, means psychologically: becoming alert and attentive.[41] Similarly, *prati-bodha*, the attainment of a (reflected = *prati*) enlightenment means psychologically: intellectual awareness.

40. Accordingly, L. de La Vallée Poussin translates *saṁ-vega,* in Vasubandhu's *Abhidharmakośa*, in chapter iii, 94, "terreur de l'existence," in chapter vi, 58. "dégoût." In chap. vi, 55, the whole psychological development of the term is given: only when this "terreur-dégo t" has arisen, one is induced to enter the path of Liberation.

41. As Professor E.H. Johnston kindly pointed out to me, there is a curious interchange in the texts between this term and *anu-bodha*; the latter seems to be used for partial comprehension by those less advanced or in relation to a subject which is not fundamental. This would agree with the general meaning of the prefix *anu*, which always indicates something secondary.

A new forward tendency is now gained. *Pra-vrajyā* is : the taking up (*pra*) the stage of the wandering mendicant. *Pra-ṇi-dhāna* is: the striving for a support, and such indicates "prayer" and results in aspiration and resolve. *Pra-buddha* is : the longing for enlightenment and thus the gaining of the psychological result of vigilance. *Pra-jñā* thus means: striving after and through this effort gaining higher intuitive knowledge. *Upa-saṁ-padā* is the striving after accomplishment and accepting as its means the ordination service.

The prefix *abhi* serves equally to express this higher tendency and results in spiritual development. *Abhi-jñā* means: striving after higher (eschatological or magical) knowledge, and at the same time is the psychological term for developing the capacity of reaching this aim. *Abhi-vinaya* means accordingly: higher discipline. *Abhi-dharma*, aiming at the essential *dharma*, designates: metaphysical *dharma*, and is higher valued than *dharma* alone (moral law) or *anu-dharma*. *Anu-dharma* is the lesser *dharma*, because the prefix *anu* indicates only the taking up of something which is already fully grasped. The terms with the prefixes of forward tendency, however, always express something which is higher, because not yet realized.

The same holds good also for terms which are formed with the prefix indicating a kind of tendency from above: *adhi*. *Adhi* indicates a higher, but not yet the reaching of the transcendental sphere. *Adhi-ṣṭhāna*, generally meaning: mastery or giving support, gains in this psychological sphere the meaning of longing for a hold which is not yet completely reached and therefore so eagerly aimed at; it means psychologically: intent, determination and thereby satisfaction. *Adhi-citta* indicates through the very process explained: higher thought; similarly, *adhi-pra-jñā* is the higher aim not yet realized; it is a preparatory step and thus gains the psychological significance of: confidence and faith. *Adhi-pati-phala* means in this context (cf. contra the explanations given in the logical sphere): the fruit of higher influence, the main tendency which determines future existences. Even if Buddhism refuses to make any positive statement about that which transgresses the sphere of actual experience, the concrete character of the lofty aim in mind is already pointed at by its actual reflection on both the ethical and psychological tendencies.

The prefix *sam* too, finds its adequate place in these psychological considerations. *Saṁ-(y)ak*, lit.: the curving together, is no more an attachment to a single object or objects, but the psychological state in which distraction in thought, feeling, and action is no more; as such it provides a necessary preparation for indifference towards the worldly struggles of opposing tendencies. Recognizing the merely momentary value of the so-called empirical goods and their inevitable change into their opposites, the evils, the Buddhist, like the Yogin, comes to the *sama*-view,[42] the indiscriminating and unattached view on all happenings. Thus, he attains the true balance and harmony of mind. *Saṁ-jñā* and *saṁ-jñāna* (cf. *saṁ-jñā*, explained from the empirical angle as collective consciousness of single facts) gains in this context the meaning of concentrated, i.e. unmoved and unmovable consciousness.

Concerning the prefixes of dispersion, they too appear in Buddhist technical terms not only in the empirical sphere but also as effective in the higher stages of development. *Vi-bhāva*, which means on the empirical level as a general term: diffused

---

42. The playing on connection of the prefix *sam* with the adjective and adverb *sama* frequently occurs in the exposition of the Yogic attitude in the *Bhagavadgītā*, e.g. 2, 15 and 2, 38. In Buddhist texts *sama* is, furthermore, intermixed with *śama*, repose, because beside their phonetical affinities both terms indicate the same psychological attitude.

wealth and prosperity, gains in the context of thoughts on renunciation the significance of removal (*vi*) of all *bhavas*, of all empirical phenomena and the attachment to them. *Vi-naya*, lit. the driving away (of obstruction), is the technical term for Buddhist preparation towards perfection. *Vi-bhaṅga* similarly means: psychological steadfastness and determination, the breaking away (*bhaṅga*), being removed(*vi*).[43]

A slightly different shade of meaning is evident in those terms where the prefix *vi* is used to enhance the meaning already implied in the rest of the compound. *Vi-ni-vṛtti* indicates: the fixing down (*ni*) of activity (*vṛtti*) corroborated by the prefix *vi*; all distracting influences are dispelled and thus a quasi-neutral psychological attitude towards the world and all its beings is gained. *Vi-ni-vṛtti* results in a general objective goodwill towards all fellow-creatures.

Nir, the prefix indicating a more forceful way of removal, is appropriately used in this sphere of determined renunciation. *Nir-hāra* means in the preliminary stage of ecclesiastical order: the removal of an unworthy priest; in its eschatological tendency it indicates the deliberate removal of all worldly ties, and such the attainment of Buddhahood. *Niḥ-svabhāva*, the eradication of singled-out being, which is originally a general logical term, gains in Buddhism a psychologico-eschatological significance as : transformed higher being, after the fiction of the *ahaṁkāra*, the principle of individualization, has been given up.

This final renunciation of the world, however, is felt as a positive tendency. Thus, here once more is the place for the application of prefixes of positive forward tendency (in case

---

43. Differently explained in the Pali Text Society's dictionary, but the above interpretation comes near to the translation of the term adopted by E.J. Thomas, *The History of Buddhist Thought*, p. 274.

the renunciation is expressed by the noun to which such prefix is added). *Abhi-niṣ-kramaṇa* means: to devote oneself (*abhi*) to the *niṣ-kramaṇa*, the abandoning of the worldly course. *Pra-hāṇa* is: the tendency (*pra*) towards giving up all worldly bondage.

The final aim, however, the actual transgression into the other sphere, into the Transcendental, is expressed by eliminating all empirical conditions. Now the determined repelling of everything which is empirical is the *conditio sine qua non*. This is illustrated by prefixes of a strong negating effort. The impulse of pushing beyond the borderline between the Empirical and Transcendental is significantly indicated. *Apa-varga* is in Buddhism, as in the Hindu systems, the pushing away (*apa*) of all limitations (*varga*) and thus indicates: deliverance.

The most characteristic terms for this final stage are formed with the prefix *nis*, which, stronger than all the others, illustrates a quasi-explosive function of dispersion. *Niḥ-saraṇa* shows the forceful way out of the *saṁ-sāra* by destroying all *sara*s, all influences. *Nir-vāṇa*, finally, indicates the function of blowing asunder all material, logical and psychological worldly matters. Substance remains, but in no possible combination of further empirical outgrowth.[44]

A last word may be added about the prefix *pari*. Though it is significantly used in the Buddhist term of *pari-nirvāṇa*, it does not bring in any further shade of meaning except the one which is its character in all spheres of its application. *Pari* indicates the encircling motion and thus enhances the completion of all that is expressed in the other parts of the compound to which it is added. In the lower spheres it is used in terms like *pari-kalpa* complete imagination or

44. See about the different aspects of *Nir-vāṇa*, my *Indian and Western Philosophy*, pp. 49, 53 f., and *Nirvāṇa*, in Modern Review, Calcutta, 1939.

construction. Logically *pari-hāra* designates: exclusion by isolation. In the psychological sphere, on the other hand, it is applied in terms like *pari-ni-vṛtta*, coming fully (*pari*) to a standstill and thus being psychologically prepared for the Nirvāṇa.

10. Jainism[45]

The most characteristic feature of Jainism with regard to the problem in hand is not what it supplies but what it lacks. There are very few keywords with prepositions prefixed, and these few are transformed according to the specific Jaina tendency. Neither should one expect to find here a multitude of simple terms instead of compounds with prefixes. Jainism, it will rather appear, is less concerned with coining new terms and investigating new problems than with classifying given facts that are already known. A great number of nouns are used which are mostly members of *dvandva*-compounds, enumerations of static aggregates. Intensity, too, is expressed in Jaina terminology not by addition of a prefix but by mere repetition of the simple term (cf. *nidrā-nidrā*, heavy sleep; *sthūla-sthūla*, extremely gross (not *ati-sthūla*), etc.)

Beings of the human, animal, and vegetable kingdoms, their specific conditions, qualities, and even their fixed measurements, are as it were just listed in a register. It is no accident that every interpreter of Jaina ideas is induced to use frequent tabular accounts. No other system suggests in such a degree this kind of treatment.

Mythological concepts about inhabitants of heaven and hell and problematic intermixture between these two extra-

45. I venture to neglect the historical question whether Buddhism or Jainism goes back to earlier times. From the methodical standpoint of this essay I am inclined to deal with Jainism later than Buddhism, because Jainism provides a kind of counter-test to the previous expositions.

empirical spheres are accepted as plain and undubitable facts, and brought into the framework of rigid measurable order. No fundamental doubts as to the different levels of reality are raised: clear-cut statements are made; phenomena are gererally treated as static facts,[46] and their obvious variations are left unquestioned; different qualities are considered only on a basis of numerical gradations. The various conditions of things are viewed as mathematical permutations (*syād-vāda*) and not as biological possibilities.

Nor is fundamental problem of dynamics generally raised:[47] even the concept of the soul does not imply for the Jaina essentially dynamic motion. The plants, the *sthāvara*s, the immovables, even stones, are included in the order of beings endowed with souls.

In accordance with this statistical and static attitude, even the liberated soul of a higher, say, a human being, is viewed from the empirical and classifying standpoint. The liberated ones are considered still to be divided into different classes with regard to their former social standings and even with reference to their former physical size and measurement (two-third of their last embodied size is assumed to be retained in the stage of deliverance). The measuring-rod of the empirical world is thus introduced for all kinds of extra- and super-empirical stages. To emphasize this rigidity of Jaina thought let me recall the fundamentally contrasting attitude of the Vedānta which conceives a formless and nameless being not only for the postulate of Liberation (cf. the well-known similes of *Chānd. Up.*, 6, 9, ff) but even views the whole empirical world as a merely relative and ever-changing reality.

46. Even actual movements and dynamics are merely acknowledged as a fixed law. Thus the peculiar Jaina use of the term *dharma*, as principle or means of motion, may be explained.

47. Cf. the preceeding note.

Temporal notions are introduced, too, in Jainism not as dynamic but as purely numerical concepts. The different periods of the world (*yugas* and *kalpas*) and the various stages of individual development and perfection are meticulously computed and fixed in numbers which, although enormously great, are still calculable numbers. As long as number, as long as Time, as long as measure and limit are acknowledged, so far the Finite is not transgressed.[48]

Jaina concepts of cosmogony and cosmology fit perfectly in this general framework. The world as a whole is another given and immutable fact. It is not created and is not perishable and has, though a great, but measurable size. It is hermetically enclosed in wind-sheaths or empty space.

Against these expositions of Jaina static classification and empirical realism[49] one may object that it is precisely this system which has fully developed theories of biological function and detailed statements on pre- and post-empirical conditions; in short, that this school is specially concerned with speculations of the *karma*-doctrine.[50] But here, too, there prevails the

---

48. As a contribution to and affirmation of the above analysis of Jaina thought, one may quote W. Schubring's striking statement (*Die Lehre der Jainas*, Leipzig, 1935, p. 108, ann.6) that the Jainas conceive the Infinite as an extremely great but still definite figure lying outside the range of human capacity of computation, but not transgressing the genus of number.

49. Realism is here understood as a teaching of measurable facts not of biological processes.

50. The most developed psychological and biological treatment of the *karma*-doctrine, however, is to be found in the expositions of *Yoga-sūtras*, 2, 13 Comm., where a threefold division is made between the *pradhāna-karma*, the main tendency which had to be fulfilled first and thus brought to an end, and the *svalpa-karma*, the small and negligible tendencies which can be overpowered, and the *upasarjana-karma*, lit. the pouring on,

statistical and realistic tendency. The psychological differences of various types of *karma* are assumed and stated as specimens of different fixed qualities and proportions and distinguishable colourings (*leśyā*). Psychological reactions are generally regarded as the mechanical increase or decrease of accumulated matter. Besides, the manifest actions of this form of embodiment are, as it were, extended backwards into a former stage of potential predispositions; the past *karma* is retrospectively seen as a calculable process. In adding to or subtracting from the present *karma* fixed numbers of degrees the past *karma* is revealed. These numbers differ according to the various *karma*-types.

Only with regard to the future is a more active, and as such a dynamical, attitude taken. A kind of counter-physics is demanded in order to counteract undesired physical results. Jainism, too, in accord with the general Indian tendency, aims at cutting off the bondage of further reincarnations. But even here the fundamental aspects of the Finite are not fully abandoned. Jainism is the only Indian system which does not object to suicide for the purpose of deliverance, and thus believes in the capacity of bringing the stream of life and *karma* abruptly to an end. If this forceful means is not used then the biological process of the development and growth of the *karma-bīja* (*karma*-seed) continues. But, nevertheless, even then in investigating this functional process there is introducted once more a static notion. The continuous process is cut into quantitative static measurements, constituent parts (*pra-deśa*s). *Karma* itself is

→ the middle tendencies, which come to their realization after the main *karma* is exhausted. These latter are like leaking taps by which liquid, the *karma*-substance, is gradually accumulated and thus increased by degrees to such an extent that it has to be finally counteracted.

taken as a concrete matter which having penetrated the soul divides itself into several parts, *karma-prakṛtis*.

In dealing now with terms which in the other systems have retained their full potentialities, I have to view their use in Jainism and to trace how much of their genuine dynamics is left when they are adapted to the general tendency of Jainism. *Prakṛti*, for instance, is here introduced not in its full functional meaning of continuous emanation, but as almost stationary and as subdivided into finite parts. *Ut-sarpiṇī* and *ava-sarpiṇī*, the original dynamic meaning of which is: evolving and revolving (periods of the world), though dynamic in expression, become static in the detailed exposition, while fixed and limited to numerical definite parts or to duration expressed in fixed numbers.

Other prefixes, too, get a static and rigid meaning in their Jainistic use: *upa-pāta*, lit. the falling towards, fig. the manifestation of extra-worldly beings, loses its dynamic sense when inserted in the general classifying order of mere existence. The Jainas are less concerned with investigating the process of manifestation itself than with its completed result. *Upa-bhoga*, though in itself *upa* is a strongly dynamic prefix of direction, seems in Jainism to be used preferably in a static sense of addition and super-imposition. The Jaina thinker takes into consideration not the act of tending forwards but once more its result, the locative sense, so to speak, of lying upon. Thus, one has to understand the term, prescribed in monastic rules, of the *upa-bhoga-pari-bhoga* (*vrata*); *pari*, like *upa*, being also taken in a merely locative sense of completion and not of encircling. *Upa-ghāta* (*nāma-karma*) is similarly applied rather in the sense of shifting one upon another, and thus of resulting in a wrong location than in the sense of forward motion, i.e. collision.

Accordingly, *nir-māṇa* means: the already distributed position of bodily members.

The prefix *prati*, too, is not used in its dynamic sense of counter-movement but in its static meaning of having established counterparts. In Jaina hagiology Nārāyaṇas or Vāsudevas are enumerated together with their opposites, the Prati-Nārāyaṇas or Prati-Vāsudevas.

As to the prefix *sam*, here, too, mostly the static meaning of construction, i.e. completion, is enhanced. *Saṁ-hanana* denotes something which is linked together; *saṁ-sthāna* is used as: fixed bodily construction; *saṁ-ghātana* (*nāma-karma*) illustrates the holding together rather than the falling together. Again, not so much the process of coming together as its result, the fact of statically lying side by side, is taken into consideration.

The same trend of thought underlies Jaina logic. The special Jaina contribution to Indian logic is the *syād-vāda* to which I had to refer already in former chapters. It gives a survey of the different conditions and possibilities of things, not from a biological but from a mathematical angle. Their variations are lineally arranged. As to single logical terms they, too, are applied in the static form of stating a fact and not presenting a process. *Ava-graha* or *ava-dhāraṇā* is for the Jaina thinker a logical perception by isolating the object under consideration from its context, so that it can be perceived as something special. *Anyath(ā)-ān-upa-patti* is here the condition for a valid logical proof by wilful classification of predicates; if only the logical operation is correctly fulfilled the result is accepted, even if it contradicts the actual biologically given qualities. *Ap(a)-āya* or *apa-gama*, lit. the going away, means for the Jaina logician: to make a statement after undesired perturbating considerations have been removed. Accordingly, *adhy-ava-sāya*, the logical term for decision, gets in Jainism the meaning of de-cision, i.e. cutting off all undesired tendencies arising from the process of the flowing in, i.e. influence, of *karma-* substance.

These last Jaina terms are on the borderline of logic and psychology.

As soon as not only an objective statement but an intentional development (with regard to the future *karma*) is wanted, some terms with prefixes are applied in which the directing power of the prefixes is still vividly felt. In this sphere the prefix *sam* gets its dynamic meaning of com-pression. *Saṁlekhanā* designates the deliberate effort of the Jaina monk towards the stopping of natural vital motion for the sake of reaching Liberation (cf. the above remark on religious suicide). *Sam-ud-ghāta* means lit. the driving out and driving together and thus, like *ā-hāraka*, illustrates the unhindered capacity of the perfect Jaina saint. He may leave his body already during lifetime of his own free will for some period and afterwards resume the conjunction of body and soul. This Jaina concept may well be contrasted with the Vedāntic assumption of the temporary giving up of the connection between *Ātman* and body. First, in Vedānta this separation takes place not in a self-willed but in a natural way (during deep sleep). Secondly, the Vedānta illustrates this assumed capacity by the smile of a bird (the soul) which, though bound to its resting place (the body) by a long string, can fly away, without completely breaking off the connection. In Jainism, on the other hand, the saint can cut his being into two (or more) separate finite existences.[51]

Dynamics, it is true, are postulated in Jainism for the sphere of *karma*, but these are never natural cosmic dynamics. It is a forcible human effort of counteracting natural processes, e.g. the *karma*-process. *Ā-srava*, the continuous flowing in,

51. Cf. *contra* also the Yogic concept of *kaivalyam*, where even the final deliverance, isolation, is still bound to a form of empirical existence as long as the natural separation between body and soul, through death, has not set in (*Yoga-sūtras*, 1, 51 Comm.)

influence, of *karma*-matter into the soul, is a natural ripening process (*vi-pāka*) of the *karma*-seed into its fruit. An equally dynamic counter-process has to be created by one who wants to escape this world of *karma*.*Vy-ut-sarga* means: the full (*vi*) *ut-sarga*, renunciation or control of bodily impulses. The natural life-force of *karma* has to be squeezed together, to be compressed (*saṁ-varaṇa*) and he who is longing for Liberation has to see to it that it withers away(*nir-jarā*). The Jaina strives to become a *nir-grantha*, i.e. one by whom the *granthas*, the fetters of empirical existence, are broken asunder. Here, in the description of biological natural action and psychological counter-action, the prefixes applied have retained some of their general emotional significance. In the terms of deliberate counter-action the explosive meaning of *nir* and the compressing power of *sam* can be made use of.

Under the same aspect the prefix *upa* also occurs in its intentional forward motion (As desired development). *Upa-śama*, not unlike the use of this term in the Yoga system (*Yoga-sūtras*, 2, 15 Comm.), means: striving after pacification, i.e. intentional suppression. *Apa-vartanā*, lit. the rolling aside, designates the intentionally accelerated realization of *karma* in order to bring it soon to an end.[52] *Ud-vartanā*, again, is its counterpart of deliberately showing down the development[52] Both are aspects of the *Ud-īraṇā*, the developement (*ud*) of *īraṇā*, the volitionary counter-force of *ud-aya*, the natural development of *karma*.

Jainism is, as I have tried to explain, on the whole satisfied with stating given facts and arranging them in a systematic order. This fixation and classification is undertaken, though

52. Cf. *Abhidhānarājendra sub verbo apa-vartanā*: *karmaparamāṇūnām dīrghasthitikālatām apagamayya hrasvasthitikālatayā vyavasthāpane*. The corresponding reverse is given *sub verbo ud-vartanā*.

apparently objectively, as an acknowledgement of the human capacity of order and discrimination. When, for this purpose, some few terms with prefixed prepositions are used, the prefixes are applied not in their dynamical function of proceeding, but in a secondary way, as if they designate the accomplished process to which they lead up to.

The prefixes appear, however, with some of their emotional expressiveness when they are used in terms referring to the theory and action of *karma*. Then, in some way, the directing power of prefixes is maintained. For here Jainism has to deal with tendencies, the biological one and the counter-tendencies mobilized against it.

The Jaina system, by its forcible tendency either to fixation or to counter-action of natural forces, throws into relief the problem of the significance of prefixes. Either it avoids the use of prefixes or it stabilizes the prefixes by denoting their results and not their proceedings; or else they are only used in one of their possible meanings. The Jaina system is most instructive for the problem of the significance of prefixes in its restricted application of their various potentialities.

It is perhaps no accident that the matter-of-fact Jaina system has appealed, in the main, to the merchant class.

3

Multiple Prefixes

As a supplement to the detailed expositions given above with reference to the various systems, let us now view the general philologico-philosophical problem of double and multiple prefixes and endeavour to trace the laws of their mutual influence. The use of double or even more prefixes in one compound presupposes a complicated and elastic manner of thinking. The linguistic expression, that is, tries to embrace all possible dynamics of co-operation and counter-forces which work on the simple noun or verb to which the prefixes are added.

As to the question whether there are certain rules which determine the use of only one or more prefixes, as applied in the formation of philosophical terms, an indication in the main tenets of the systems themselves can be found. It does not seem accidental that those systems which take into consideration internal and external action, re-action and cross-action between the ontological and psychological spheres are more inclined to apply double and multiple prefixes. They try to express the divergent movements and various conditions of things. The multiplicity of prefixes serve their purpose by throwing into relief all possibilities of functions (cf. e.g. the above remarks on the Yoga system). Other philosophical schools, however, which look at the phenomena from a preconceived scope which limits their range into one direction only, exclude complicated counter-movements. Thus, the latter generally prefer terms with but one prefix, or use a combination of prefixes the functions of which corroborate each other when in collaboration.

Before starting to investigate the mutual influences excercised by multiple prefixes one has to recall the functions of prefixes in general.

As appears from the above examples taken from the various systems they are as it were dynamos, genuine *gatis*. They draw the verb or noun to which they are yoked in the direction of their respective movements; and a combination of these forward tractors (like *abhy-upa; anu-pra*, or in vertical corroboration, e.g. *ava-ni*), accelerate, so to speak, the speed and intensity of the course taken. This motion is, however, restrained or even trapped, when one prefix designating forward motion is counteracted by another prefix which works in another, say, backward, direction, like *vy-ati, praty-upa*, etc. A third variety occurs when the prefix which pulls in the forward direction is brought to a standstill (in case of equal intensity), i.e. when the horizontal pull is counterbalanced by another prefix functioning on the vertical line (*ava, ni, ut,* etc.).

And if one among several prefixes is predominant then, too, a variety of possibilities can be observed. In general, the first in position is the strongest of the "team" of prefixes; it overpowers the functioning of the prefixes following in the series and pulls the noun or verb, "the cart" so to speak, in its direction. A second variety arises when the later prefixes have more or less lost their independent dynamics and are little more than the foremost part of the "chassis" (in plain words: when the prefixes nearest to their verb or noun form together with it one already fixed concept). Then the first prefix moves the whole in its own direction.

These varieties of operations, co-operations and counter-operations of dynamically felt prefixes are fully employed in Sanskrit, and far more favoured than in any other language of the Indo-European group. The first reasons for this Sanskrit characteristic are the fundamental concepts to be traced everywhere in Hindu thought: that of dynamics and that of traditionalism. Another reason, too, is based on general Hindu thought and mirrored in Hindu linguistics. The peculiar Hindu view of juxtaposition which I ventured to point out for Sanskrit grammar[1] has developed the unique Sanskrit use of long compounds. A species of this Hindu predilection for compounds can be seen in the tendency for compilation of prefixes in such a multitude as is neither found nor considered so perfectly natural anywhere else in the Indo-European languages.[2]

Another Hindu law of thinking, however, hampers our effort to bring the functioning of prefixes under clear-cut Western systematics: Hindu terms are essentially vague and ambiguous[3] and the same holds good for the significance of their prefixes. As life itself cannot be restrained by chains of theory the prefixes also which are never deadened are not to be grasped by one theoretical law alone.

Nevertheless, I venture to trace the essential features of multiple combined prefixes through the following considerations. How can we find some kind of systematic

---

1. Cf. my "Zur Psychologie der indischen Grammatik", *Archiv Orientální*, 1935.
2. In ancient Greek, it is true, there is also occasionally found a compilation of more than two prefixes. This, however, is generally to be met with, at any rate in later Greek, in authors whose style is regarded as entangled and artificial.
3. Cf., e.g. my *Indian and Western Philosophy*, *passim*, especially the "Index of Problems Treated", p. 155. The very ambiguity leads to divergent fixed meanings within the framework of the different systems.

order for the relationship between the members of such complicated compounds ? What are the ways of interconnection between these prefixes themselves and between the prefixes and the noun to which they are added?

As to the relation between the prefixes themselves, there are two aspects of this: their interconnection when viewed from the angle of their contents and, secondly, when viewed from the degree of their respective intensity. Their mutual influence represents itself either as an additional corroborative function, or as a modifying force (co-ordinative or successive), or as a counteracting motion. As to the second question about their graded intensity, the stress lies either on the first or on one of the following prefixes. I shall only touch incidentally on this problem; in analysing the different members of the compound and tracing the predominance of the function of the one prefix for the meaning of the whole, the question of relative intensity will be implicitly answered.

Coming to the second inquiry one touches once more on a complicated problem rarely to be encountered in any other Indo-European language. Here one is dealing with the relationship by which one or two prefixes stand in a more intimate connection with the noun than the rest of the prefixes. It is a fact that the process of the growing together of prefix and noun into a static unity is developed much further in other language than in Sansksrit. This coalescence is with the others only the result of a weakening of the dynamics of prefixes in general. This weakening, however, never happens in Sanskrit, as is evident from two decisive considerations. First, it is not always the prefix nearest to the noun which forms an already fixed concept with it. I shall give later an example of the opposite process. Secondly, the compound is changed frequently in its meaning by the predominant prefix, either in a negating or in a supplementing sense (if the complex implied already in itself a negation).[4] The full functional meaning of the complex to be negated is, however, still vividly felt; otherwise a merely logical negation (*a*) could be applied. Instead of it, however, the prefixes *vi, nir*, and *apa* are used, which suggest a dispersing function. Negation must be expressed by altering the direction of the original primary motion, as contained in the meaning of the noun and the other prefix more nearly related to it. The Sanskrit compounds are still alive in their functional meaning, therefore dynamic negations are preferably used.

As to the first group of prefixes to be taken into consideration: on account of the similarity of their tendencies these prefixes work in intensified corroboration, i.e. with accumulated force.[5]

Abhy-upa-gama means: to grasp and to accept. *Abhi-praṇaya* is: firm devotion. *Nir-vy-ūḍha* means: fully demonstrated, i.e. carried out in all divergent directions.

4. The riddle of the sometimes even contradictory meanings of one and the same prefix proffered in our modern Western Sanskrit dictionaries may perhaps be thus solved: the prefix remains unchangeable in itself but its meaning differs according to its context. A prefix of negative meaning attached to a verbal root of negative meaning generally gains a corroborating sense. More striking is the fact that prefixes like *vi* and *nir* have sometimes a corroborating function when connected with a verbal root of not expressly negative significance. *Nir-baddha* means: bound-together (*baddha*) so firmly that it crushes (*nir*) the thing. *Vi-ṣṭambha*, on the other hand, means support (*stambha*) in all possible directions (*vi*). In neither case is the prefix *nir* or *vi* viewed in its usual centrifugal function: it functions here in an inverted order as a centripetal motion.

5. Pāṇini, 1,4,93, gives a strange explanation of this corroborating process of combining similar prefixes. In the compounds *adhy-ā-gacchati* and *pary-ā-gacchati* the prefixes *adhi* and *pari* are called *an-arthakau*. This should not be translated as "meaningless", but as "without a (special) tendency". This interpretation, suggested by the context, is in accord with the original meaning of the root *arth*, to strive after. Later grammarians, like the author of the *Vākyapadīyam*, give a similar explanation to that suggested by the present writer.

Vy-apa-deśa represents yet another group. Here, the combination of two prefixes of similar though not the same tendency works in corroborative and specifying function; its meaning is: detailed demonstration, while pointing out the various divergent ways of exposition. *Abhi-vy-añjana* means: distinctive and intentional (*abhi*) manifestation. *Abhi-vy-āpti* is: universal pervasion, all-inclusion. Here the intentional approach (*abhi*) is worked through (*vi*) in all logical ways of investigation.

Adhy-ā-hāra is: supplying a new supposition, and thus is a more specified expression for systematic theorem than *adhi-karaṇa*, the term with the single prefix.

Vy-ā-khyā is: detailed explanation; here the prefix *vi* does not negate, but specifies the meaning of *ā-khyā*. The approach (*ā*) is traced in all its possibilities. *Vy-ā-pāra* means: proceeding; the forward tendency is worked out in all directions.

Vi-pra-kīrṇa then also expresses, by the dynamics of its prefixes, the completion of forward movements in different directions. *Vi-pra-kīrṇa* is: fully scattered, i.e. the forward motion of *pra* is supplemented and corroborated (in the sense of its simple term) by the radiating force of *vi*.

A slightly different significance of the combination of *vi* and *ā* is found in the term *vy-ā-moha*, complete illusion or confusion; it indicates diversion, non-concentration, which is already implied in the simple noun *moha*. *Vi* and *ā* underline the unsteadiness, the seeking hither and thither for escape. Here, we have a case where both prefixes enhance the immanent meaning of the simple noun.

After these examples of double prefixes which corroborate each other in their functions those double prefixes which modify each other in their action are to be viewed. *Sam-ā-patti* means : accidental connection; the prefix *ā* illustrates the accidental forward motion, while *sam* supplies the comprehensive force. To the same group belongs *saṁ-pra-yoga*, union and tendency to union. Here, the prefix *pra* emphasizes the impetus and *sam* corroborates the meaning of the noun.

Next an example of the co-operation of two prefixes which supplement each other as successive stages. *Upa-niṣ-krama* means the religious rite of taking a child out for the first time. Here, *upa,* the making up of one's mind for this purpose, is followed by the *niṣ* (*-krama*). In a similar manner the Buddhist term *abhi-niṣ-krama* may be explained.

An interesting study is to observe the mutual influences of prefixes, when even more than two are co-operating. *Abhi-vy-ā-haraṇa* means: designation. The object to be grasped, *haraṇa,* is approached first in a general forward direction (*ā*) which spreads out (*vi*) and is then definitely seized by a second intentional impulse (*abhi*). In this case all the corroborating prefixes function in a successive order.

Here is yet another kind of dynamic influence between prefixes, illustrating not the additional, not the modifying force, not the successive stages but a kind of counter-action between prefixes. The representative prefixes for this process are *vy-ati, ati-vi,* and *prati* (the latter combined with various prefixes either preceding or succeeding it).

Vy-ati-ṣaṅga, vy-ati-hāra, and *vy-ati-kara,* all designate: reciprocity, exchange; similarly *vy-ati-krama* means: inversion. Thus, it appears that the combination of *vi* and *ati* gives the noun or verb to which they are added the significance of a reverse action. I shall try to explain this from the very meaning of the prefixes in question. *Ati,* the going beyond, is caught in its tendency by *vi,* the dispersing function which breaks like a reflector the unhindered forward motion (*ati*) and throws it back. It is noteworthy, however, that this process takes place, as it were, outside the limited space, i.e. after *ati* has led beyond the sphere of finite ground. Though the prefix *ati* is one of the strongest in function, it is here counteracted by the prefix *vi.*

A somewhat different process is illustrated in the term *vy-ati-reka*. This frequently applied term has, even in the sphere of definite logic, retained a kind of ambiguity. Either the prefix *vi* is felt as stronger in this combination and then the meaning is : difference or exclusion; or *ati* is taken as prevalent and then *vy-ati-reka* is used in the sense of "surpassing". The two prefixes are here not taken as co-operating successively or simultaneously, but alternatively.

The combination of the prefixes *vi* and *ati* occurs also in reverse order : *ati-vi*; but then the union gains quite a different meaning; a significant test for the undeadened dynamics of prefixes, even when used in combination. With this latter group of compounds I shall deal later in another context.

The classical prefix for counter-movement is *prati*. Whatever its position among the combined prefixes, it predominates in its function. *Vi-prati-kāra*, for instance, means: counteraction (predominant *prati*, though not given the first place). The same is the case in terms like *vi-prati-patti*. *Vi-prati-patti* means: mutual (*prati*) discrepancy (*vi-patti*), or even mutual (*prati*) relation. In the latter case the prefix *vi* is fully overpowered by *prati*. *Praty-ā-kṣepa*, on the other hand, provides room for the working of both prefixes in a successive order. Its meaning is: jeering at, i.e. first attacking (*ā*) and then repulsing (*prati*).

The functioning of these prefixes can be explained similarly, though somewhat differently, in terms like *praty-ā-satti*. The double function of at first a forward motion (*ā*) and then a second motion of *prati* as a reacting, and thus backward driving, force may be found in *praty-ā-satti*. Its meaning is thus: analogy, a reciprocal association between two objects.

A slightly different group is represented by *saṁ-prati-patti*, Here, *prati* is not alone decisive, but represents a preliminary stage to the functioning of *sam*. *Saṁ-prati-patti* means: final agreement. Here, the resulting agreement is reached when all the *contras* (*prati-patti*) and all the *pros* (*saṁ-patti*) have been considered.

In the combination of more than two prefixes one of the series gets generally a leading significance. If *prati* is one of this "team" it mostly overpowers the other prefixes. Thus *prati-sam-ā-dhāna* means: cure (by antidote), the two other prefixes merely designating the efforts taken, the tendency (*ā*) and concentrated deliberate will (*sam*) to find the desired remedy. One may compare this term with terms like *prati-sam-āsana*, coping with.

Now to those groups in which prefixes work from different directions, from the horizontal and the vertical. They have to be separated from the preceding cases in which *prati* was traced as counter-action, but functioned in the same horizontal plane with its following prefixes.

saṁ-ni-dhi means : disposition, arrangement of a sentence; fixation (*ni*) and connection (*sam*). Here, both prefixes, the horizontally (*sam*) and the vertically working (*ni*) corroborate each other while functioning successively. The same is the case with *vy-ut-thāna*. It indicates great activity or opposition or upheaval, while rising forth (*ut*) and spreading out (*vi*). Similarly, *vy-ava-sāya*, perseverance, exertion, and determination, is a term where a derivative of the root *sā*, to bind, is combined with the prefixes *ava* (fixing down) and *vi* (the working in all different directions). Thus are illustrated efforts that are fixed and all-penetrating (cf. the above remarks on the Yoga system).

Somewhat different are the terms in which *upa* and *ni* are prefixed. Here, the second is conceived as later in the process than the first one, though the former is not combined with the noun as a fixed concept. First it is the approach (*upa*) and then the setting down (*ni*) that is taken into consideration. *Upa-ni-ṣad*, for instance, means lit. the tendency towards an object (of veneration) and the following desire to come to rest near it (*ni-ṣad*).[6] *Upa-ny-āsa*, on the other hand, seems to suggest the reverse process. *Upa-ny-āsa* means : allusion, reference, i.e. the object is at first secured (*ni*) and then it is hinted at (*upa*).

Upa-ni-kṣepa represents a group in which the two prefixes do not function in equal intensity. *Upa-ni-kṣepa* means: deposit. Here the *ni* is more accentuated than the preliminary stage of the approach (*upa*).

Vy-ava-sthā, settlement, shows also the prevalence of one prefix: *ava*. The stage of disagreement (*vi-sthā*) is overcome. *Vi-sthā*, however, cannot be regarded as a deadened complex; the function of the noun, standing, and prefix *vi*, disagreement, and prefix *ava*, to find a settlement, illustrate three successive stages of a dynamically felt process.

In some cases the prefixes of the horizontal and the vertical directions do not work in a successive order, but merely corroborate each other in the function of fixing the object on a definite crossing-point of vertical and horizontal movements. *Praty-ava-marśa* means: profound meditation. Here the fixation is reached by forward or backward motion (*prati*) which is finally fixed by *ava*.[7] *Saṁ-ni-veśa* is : deep devotion and attachment; *saṁ-ni-hita* means: lying close and firmly; *saṁ-ny-āsa*, the Yogic term, indicates complete and irrevocable renunciation of the distractions of the world.

---

6. For the above interpretation cf. Śaṅkara's remarks on *upāsana* to *Taitt. Up.* Śikṣādhyāya, 3, 4, and 12, 1. For further instances of *upa-sad* and *up(a)-ās* see my review of E. Senart, "Bṛhadāraṇyaka Upaniṣad", *J.R.A.S.*, 1937, pp. 501 ff.

7. As Professor E.H. Johnston pointed out to me, this term may also indicate "thinking back over one's past births". The looking back on past times implies a survey. Thus, in this case, implicitly, and not for the sake of fixation, the crossing point of both the horizontal and vertical movements is reached. Other uses of the term are enumerated in E.H. Johnston's translation of the *Saundarānanda*, p. 67, note.

In *saṁ-ni-yoga* and *saṁ-ni-bandha* the meaning of the simple noun is strongly enhanced by the concentrating force of *sam* (working on the horizontal line) and of the vertically fixing down of *ni*. As such *saṁ-ni-bandha* and *saṁ-ni-yoga* illutrate absolute union.

Slightly different is the meaning of terms like: *abhi-ni-veśa* and *adhy-ava-sāya*. *Abhi-ni-veśa* means: complete attachment; *abhi* expressing the tendency and *ni* emphasizing the meaning of the noun *veśa*. *Adhy-ava-sāya* shows the tendency of tackling (*adhi*) and *ava-sāya* (root *sā*) the definite settling down; its meaning is therefore: fixed determination or settling of purpose. Accordingly, *adhy-ava-sāna* means in rhetorics: complete identification of two things.

An interesting example of the divergency and non-limitation which, too, may result from the combination of horizontally and vertically functioning prefixes is represented by terms like *vy-ut-krama*. *Vy-ut-krama* means: trangression; while *ati* alone suffices to suggest transgression in the linear dimension, the combination of the dispersing power of *vi* (horizontally) and of *ut*, the upwards functioning prefix, serves to grasp the concept of spatial transgression. This is another significant example of the dynamic nature of Hindu thought. They are not satisfied with conceiving transgression merely as a linear process, but have to see it also as a complicated spatial function. *Saṁ-ni-pāta*, finally, represents a group where the horizontal and vertical functions are seen as a violent encounter of motions in Space. *Saṁ-ni-pāta*, is a most pregnant and dynamic expression of "collision". Here, not the prefixes alone but also the noun (from *pat*, to fall) co-operate to bring about the dashing together from all directions.

Now I turn to the last question to be dealt with in this chapter: to the variable relationship between noun (verb) and its prefixes.

The foregoing arguments were concerned with the independent prefixes, that is with those which are not fully grown together with the noun into a kind of solidified compound. Even where an apparently unchangeable unity between the noun and one of the prefixes has been established, the abstraction has never gone so far as in other languages. Some proofs of this have been given in the preliminary remarks of this chapter.

In dealing above with the functioning of prefixes I have already occasionally pointed out cases in which either both or one of the prefixes enhanced the meaning implied in the noun. There, the prefixes do not vary, but intensify the meaning of the noun. Now I add a few examples where part of the compound is a fixed concept in itself which is changed by the direction of the one prefix which functions freely. *Vi-pra-laya* is: complete destruction; the prefix *vi* emphasizes the dynamics of the complex formed by noun and second prefix. In the term *vi-pra-kṛti* the prefix *vi*, so to speak, hinders the forward motion (*pra* and *kṛ*) and as thus the term *vi-pra-kṛti* expresses the meaning: injury, distraction of the natural force of growth (*pra-kṛti*). The dispersive power of *vi* is effective in *vy-abhi-cāra*: deviation from the given direction, while *abhi* with *cāra* combined designates the forward motion.

As to some examples with the prefix *nir*, this leading prefix corrects, as it were, or destroys the function of the complex of noun and second prefix. *Nir-vi-kalpa* is logically: the destroying of doubts (*vi-kalpa*), and as such means: invariability; epistemologically and psychologically it is therefore: exclusive concentration, a consciousness which does not function separately any more. *Nir-vi-cikitsā* illustrates the same process; *nir-vi-cikitsā* and *nir-vi-cāra* are accordingly: definite settlement, where no further deliberation is needed. Here, the destructive meaning of *nir* gains a positive sense, while counteracting the negative meaning implied in the primary compound. *Nir-vi-*

śeṣa means in a similar manner: indiscrimination. In the various philosophical systems it is either viewed favourably or unfavourably with regard to their main tenet.

Ati-vy-āpti means: an unwarranted extension of a definition; the correct implication, *vy-āpti*, is transgressed.

Praty-av(a)-āya, on the other hand, once more shows a significant ambiguity. Either it means: contrariety (predominant *prati*) or: decrease (prevalent *ava*). It is noteworthy that even in the seemingly fixed compound *av(a)-āya* the connection is still loose enough to allow that the prefix *ava* can occasionally function freely, as it were, of its own accord (e.g. when meaning: decrease) and thus overpower the stong and leading prefix *prati*.

There are in Sanskrit very few indisputable examples of the process generally acknowledged in the other Indo-European languages by which the dynamic meaning of one or more prefixes is submerged in one abstract and fixed concept together with the noun.

Furthermore, it is no accident that the few examples, given all contain a negation, expressed by the one leading prefix, of the following complex of noun and second prefix.

As mentioned in the preliminary remarks of this chapter, all these negating prefixes like *vi, nir, apa, prati* and *ati* designate digression or trangression, in short, a deviating process. The dynamics of the negating first prefix suggests that it has to counteract another dynamic force still vividly felt in the complex of the other prefix and noun.

To sum up this chapter: Indian language and each single member of a word is a living organism — as it were — which cannot just be removed and destroyed with impunity. This is the inner reason why a verbal injury in Hindu law is nearly as much punishable as a corporeal injury.

4

Appendix
The Significance of Simple Terms

In the preceding sections I have tried to point out the significance of the prefix or prefixes in Sanskrit philosophical terminology. It may be objected, however, that the verb itself and its derivative, the noun, have in Sanskrit sufficient potentialities of meaning not to need an additional dynamic factor (the prefixes).[1] There are verbal roots and simple nouns which imply in themselves sufficient dynamics and tendencies and can, as such, be used simply as significant philosophical keywords.

While surveying the pregnant philosophical terms expressed by simple nouns or verbs we have to keep in mind some fundamental distinctions: there are genuine primary terms arising from merely methodical considerations and secondary terms which being originally artistic metaphorical expressions, become later keywords within the framework of systematics.

In the Nyāya system the term *māna*, measuring, is significantly used. Though it is frequently prefixed by *anu*, *pra*,

1. This question I raised in my "Deutung und Bedeutung indischer Terminologie", *Proceedings of the International Congress of Orientalists*, Rome, 1935; in my "Zur Psychologie der indischen Grammatik", *Archiv Orientální*, 1935, and in my "Terms *in statu nascendi* in the *Bhagavadgītā*", *New Indian Antiquary*, 1940. — After having finished this MS. I recently dealt again with these problems in "Form not" 'apart', but 'a part' of Meaning" (*University of Ceylon Review*, 1947-48).

and *upa,* it appears either in verbal form or as a noun, also as a simple term. *Mā,* to measure with the measuring-rod of human reasoning, is the chief task to which Nyāya is devoted. Besides, terms with the roots *bhid* and *chid,* to split, either as simple terms or with prefixes are favoured by the Nyāya in its analytic tendency — *Bhrānti,* lit. the flickering and erring, is depreciated as logical error.

Kāṅkṣā (*ā-kāṅkṣā*), lit. the desire, longing, or postulate, means, either with or without the prefix (*ā*), both in grammar and logic: the absence of a word necessary to complete the sense, i.e. the syntactical connection.

Sat-kārya (*vāda*) is a significant Sāṁkhya term indicating the doctrine that the *kārya* (the product) is already potentially existent (*sat*) in its cause.

Besides these methodical terms there are "descriptive" terms which are not properly systematic, but merely illustrative as examples of their group.

As such, they are pregnant with dynamics, without the addition of prefixes. I may recall the Jaina term of *syād-vāda.* The verbal form, *syād,* expresses the various possible conditions of a thing with regard to its own different stages and to its relationship with other objects.

In a similar manner *kurvad-rūpa* is in the Brāhmaṇas a descriptive grammatical term for the present tense. As Faddegon (*The Vaiśeṣika System,* p. 12) asserts, it becomes secondarily in the later Buddhist dogma a genuine term for the mere transitoriness of all objects. The solely present tense, i.e. non-permanence, is the only form of existence which such dogma acknowledges.

Another group of terms formed by simple verbs or nouns are the ambiguous terms.Verbs like *khyā* and *cakṣ* are applied even in all classical systematics in their early function of ambiguous meaning. *Khyā* and *cakṣ* designate both: to see and to speak. *Varṇa*, again, signifies: colour and sound.[2]

Throughout all systems there are a few verbal roots repeatedly occurring either in simple terms or in compounds, which have, however, in accord with the complicated Hindu manner of thought, a variety of tendencies, in spite of their simple designation. For instance, the root *man* is concerned either with our thinking- or will-power (*manas*).

Besides, some verbal roots which in general are accepted as being fully fixed and definitely terminological, retain their ambiguous meaning, even in those late systems where they have become the very keywords. *Yuj* and *muc*, the decisive terms of the Yoga system, are not deadened in *Yoga-sūtras* to their clear-cut meanings of yoga and of *mukti*, deliverance. *Yoga-sūtras*, 3, 22 Comm., speak of a fire as *mukta* that is unloosed and not guarded when *yukta* (in contact) with a breeze.[3]

Another group of ambiguous terms may be presented by the following examples. *Bhū* (*bhavati*) designates either the static statement of mere "being" or, in a sense nearer to its original meaning (cf. Latin *fu-i*), suggests dynamic development. Some roots, as well as terms derived from them, like *grah*, to grasp, *nam*, to bend, *vr̥t*, to proceed, *kl̥p*, to produce, are at times used as deadened auxiliary verbs; but more often they are conceived still in their dynamic functions. *Dhā* and *sthā*, position and disposition, are mostly still pregnant with their original meaning and as such are applied in their full physical and epistemological sense.

And yet another kind of ambiguity of simple terms may be pointed out. The vague pregnancy (*contradictio in adiecto*)

2. Further examples of terms embracing different sense-functions are given in my *Polarity of the Indefinite*, Coomaraswamy Jubilee Volume, 1938, pp. 91 ff.

3. I have treated this in greater detail in "Terms *in statu nascendi*".

of a simple term is fitted into, and fixed within, the different systems in accord with their respective tendency. Yoga means literally "union". As such it supplies a term in the different systems; it is in astronomy: a conjunction of stars; in arithmetics: addition; in grammar: etymological association. *Yogyatā*, its derivative, acquires in the Nyāya the sense of applicability, i.e. absence of absurdity in the mutual connection, compatibility of sense; as a specific yoga term it designates fitness for yogic meditation. *Sādhanā*, lit. fulfilment, is in Nyāya the solution of a problem, i.e. proof; in yoga: psychological perfection.

Besides the above-mentioned proper terms based on rational deductions, there have to be viewed some metaphorical terms in which the rational application for systematics is only secondary. The Sāṁkhya introduces for the *prakṛti* the significant designation *nartakī*, the (cosmic) dancer. Her name, *nartakī*, illustrates in a nutshell the main dogma of the Sāṁkhya. Just as the so-called theistic schools denote the creation of the world performed by a God as a kind of *līlā*, the free play of His creative or destructive power, in the same way *prakṛti* dances before the *puruṣa*, in a voluntary display of her dynamic capacities.

In a similar manner the Vedānta provides some suggestive metaphorical expressions. Based on transcendental vision, it tries to illustrate super-empirical concepts by comparisons taken from simple everyday life. Very much in contrast to the use of a metaphor in poetry, the metaphor is here always taken from a lower sphere than the subject to which it is being applied. Not an elevation but rather a degradation is intended, in order to render perceptible those notions which are by their very manner of conception inaccessible to the sensory faculties. *Sākṣin*, lit. the spectator, designates the super-mundane *Ātman* or *Brahman*. *Kūṭa-stha*, lit. standing across and protruding and thus not fitting into any empirical framework, is a figurative term for the immovable or uncontrollable supreme *Ātman*.[4] *Bhoktṛ*, lit. the enjoyer, and *kṣetrin*, lit. the owner of the field, are metaphors for the individual *Ātman*. *Jaḍa*, lit. blunt, is a pregnant expression for unconscious Matter (in the Vedānta[5] and Sāṁkhya). *Bhūmis*, lit. the grounds, gain in the yoga the significance of the different stages of perfection.[6]

In addition to all these proper terms or secondary terms which express the tendencies of the various systems, I must refer in passing to yet another group of pregnant simple verbs or nouns which, though dynamical, are not rationally tendentious. As I tried to point out in several of my essays, e.g. in my "Deutung und Bedeutung indischer Terminologie", onomatopoeia is in Sanskrit a foremost cause of the formation of words and is still more vividly felt and used than in any other highly developed language. Onomatopoeia is by its very nature the expression of dynamic function. The sound imitates the activity itself.

To conclude: both verbs and their derivations the nouns have still retained, even in the classical philosophical systems of India, their elasticity and ambiguity. Though preferably they are modified by the means of added prefixes, they are still, even as simple verbs or nouns, alive enough to embrace in themselves a variety of dynamic functions.

---

4. This original meaning is still in use in late Vedānta texts, e.g. Pañcadaśī, 6, 18-22, cf. T.M.P. Mahadevan, *Philosphy of Advaita*, London, 1939, p. 176.

5. But Gauḍapāda, the Vedāntin, uses it also in the positive sense of making oneself insensitive to the distractions of the world.

6. Original metaphors thus become, by their very suitability for expressing doctrinal concepts, secondarily technical terms for the systems concerned.

5

Epilogue
Comparison of the Technical Terms of Philosophy and Poetry

In dealing with the philosophical schools of India I have omitted the Alaṅkāraśāstram, though this, too, may be considered as a system of logic, rhetoric being the systematics of formal expression. But from our very problem of the significance of prefixes in Indian terminology we arrive at a fundamental distinction between rhetoric and the genuine philosophical schools.

First, rhetoric, as it were, is essentially a kind of secondary system based on language already selected and thus limited by artistic considerations. As such, the Alaṅkāraśāstram has not to classify the wide range and free choice of linguistic expression as its nearest relative among the philosophical schools, the system of Grammar, has to do. Rhetoric adopts laws already established by poetry. Hence, we must first investigate the attitude of poetry towards our problem, before we can form conclusions as to the significance of prefixes in the terminology of Rhetoric.

At first sight it might be expected that in the vivid language of poetry especially prefixes would play a prominent part, but a detailed study of the presuppositions and ends of poetry will reveal that this is not and cannot be the case.

The former expositions have made it clear that terms with

prefixes, more than simple terms themselves, throw into full relief certain principles of Indian mentality: India's dynamic way of thinking, her combination of rational means with irrational tendencies, her ambiguity of expression and predilection for classification which, however, is kept elastic and unfixed by the drawing of subtle distinctions.[1]

Poetry, too, takes into consideration all these general principles of dynamics, the intermixture of irrationalism and rationalism, ambiguity, fixation, and oscillating expression. But in poetry from the very outset these fundamental laws are looked at from a different angle to what they are in religion and philosophy.

Something dynamic is essential too, to poetry. Especially Indian poetry with its preference for lyrics[2] is concerned chiefly with emotion roused in the poet himself and conferred through the medium of his creations to his audience. Thus, the nine (or ten) *rasas*, sentiments, lit. tastes, underlie all poetry. Besides, movements are revealed by the poetical forms of metre, verse, or alliteration. As to its content, poetry is vividly illuminated by *śleṣas*, intertwined meanings, or by application of similes and metaphors bearing more on comparisons of functions than on static qualities. But all these dynamics contained in the poet's work are only means, not ends in themselves; besides, they are set into a fixed framework in accord with the poet's artistic plans.

Irrationalism and rationalism, too, are differently applied in poetry and in philosphical systems; here they change places, as it were, with regard to starting-point and end. In a way, Indian poetry has — paradoxically as it sounds — less dynamic

1. Cf. the remarks above on fixation through context accompanied by ambiguity, p. 93.
2. Lyrics are predominant even in the so-called dramatic art of India.

sweep than the rational systems. The creative urge of the poet is an irrational starting-point, but its resulting artistic expression is fixed and limited by the master's arbitrating order;[3] his rhythmic creations and dynamic similes are, so to speak, rationed, restricted by the poet's artistic sense, and are, for him, only means.

The poet's personality brings in at the beginning that which is the end of the philosophical systems: the super-empirical elevation. The experience of unity precedes and does not follow the phenomena. Dynamic force, unlimited dynamic force, is given only in the creative personality of the poet. From his own experience of cosmic unity, which lies before his creation, the poet establishes correspondences in the different spheres of empirical being: human, animal, vegetable and atmospheric phenomena provide him with subjects of comparison. Though these are viewed by him in some of their dynamic aspects, their natural possibilities have not a free play: only those which fit into his artistic intentions are accepted and indicated.

The poet fixes them, so to speak, on a plane apportioned by him. To us a simile: he lets them swing only in a limited sphere of circular motion between the ends of a rope which he has fastened on both sides, the pegs of his framework. "Une oeuvre d'art est un coin de la création vu à travers un tempérament," says Zola. The tendencies of the philosophical systems, on the other hand, operate like arrows; they are bound only at their starting-points, the viewpoints of the systems, and from there they fly forth unhindered in the

---

3. One can go even further. The inspiration of the Indian poet, like that of all Indian artists, is in a way already restricted in the very moment of conception by pre-established external rules and limited by traditional prescriptions. He cannot create freely but is bound to create according to models, unchangeable types. About this, see in greater detail my *Indian and Western Philosophy*, pp. 100 ff.

forward motion, and the more so the more the missile was first strictly fixed. They tend towards the aim of their system, which is preconceived in intention but not yet established.

The innate tendencies of a philosophical school are represented for the scholar by its terms, its keywords. Like a key they are used to unlock something which lies beyond. They are rational means to irrational ends. They are aiming forwards with unbroken dynamics. Though fixed in their direction, they are left to the free development of their inner potentialities.

The poet has no use for such terms of distinct independent tendencies. His irrational ends lie in his own starting-point. He knows beforehand how far he will reach. No simple terms, then, and no compound-terms which by the application of prefixes denote the various ways of approach to an aim which is hinted at but yet not realized, can play a decisive part in poetry.

Ambiguity, too, as expressed in Indian poetry, has an origin and aim other than that manifest in Indian philosophical thought. Neither a seeking of approach on different paths nor arrows shot from different bows, i.e. viewpoints, but a richness of expression to emphasize the subtly intertwined texture of his own closed network, this characterizes the poet's attitude towards multiformity. Not any divergent tendency, not any genuine ambiguity, but an ordered variability is the artistic means.

From all these considerations one may now understand the fact that comparatively few prefixes are applied in Indian poetry, and that these do not occur in prominent keywords. It is true that the prefix *pra* is frequently used with poets like Kālidāsa as a kind of motor of static adjectives (cf., e.g. *pra-*

agra, pra-tanu, pra-bala, etc.)[4] This use is an artistic addition to stress the meaning of the adjective itself and to give it a form not common to average language and to provide it with a more unusual and thus more precious touch.

Other prefixes like *ut* are preferably applied with verbal adjectives (past participles), e.g. *ut-phulla, ut-khāta*. Here, the prefix *ut* is used in its primary biological meaning of spontaneously budding forth or dynamically digging up and casting forth; but it is limited to its original biological sense and does not ascend into a metaphorical sphere. Besides, these adjectives and past participles are but secondary attributes of the noun to which they are added; they are merely descriptive supplements. As to the noun itself, it, too, never gets the pregnancy of a technical term; it may attain the function of a simile; but the difference between a technical term and a metaphor or simile lies in the fact that the simile and its abbreviated form, the metaphor, both have their significance in their relation to something else as counterparts; furthermore, the comparison effaces to a certain degree the strict contour of the object in hand. When compared to each other both objects of the comparison lose, in a way, their individual being by an oscillating mutual relationship. This relationship, it is true, is often in the simile expressed in a form suggesting dynamic counter-movements. Daṇḍin, in his *Kāvyādarśa*, 2, 57 ff., supplies a list of synonyms for expressing likeness which contains, besides merely comparative particles, verbs and nouns with or without prefixes indicating imitation, reflection, rivalry, contempt, etc. (e.g. *ni-bhā, saṁ-ni-bhā, pra-kāśa, prati-bimba, prati-garjati, ava-jānāti, ni-ṣedhati, vi-gr̥hṇāti, ā-*

4. Perhaps the prefix *pra* plays, on the whole, a predominant part among all prefixes. It seems not to be accidental that the Indian grammarians use the descriptive term *pr (a)-ādi, pra,* etc. as the prototype for all prefixes, because *pra* represents both not only the intentional but also the mechanical forward motion.

krośati). But these are merely metaphorical designations of comparison. As such, they do not actually separate the two members of the simile, nor are they in themselves independent dynamic terms, for the movements which they describe take place in a limited and definite sphere between the objects of the poet's choice.

A genuine technical term, on the other hand, remains unique and self-complete in its direction, while tending forwards towards an aim which is not yet reached.

Some philosophical systems, one may object, also make frequent use of similes. But, though doing so, they never neglect to apply genuine technical terms as well. The Vedānta, for instance, provides a number of elaborately worked-out similes.[5] Their illustrating function is here rooted in the Vedāntic dogma of cosmic unity. This system seems to approach the principles of poetry in so far that the Vedānta, too, takes cosmic unity as its starting-point; but, nevertheless, it needs genuine technical terms and tendencies; for primary unity is veiled in empirical life and must be uncovered and thus recovered at the end.

The Sāṁkhya, on the other hand, can make use only of metaphors, not of similes. *Prakr̥ti,* viewed as a cosmic dancer, is unique in her position and her emanations are graded; no equals are at hand for establishing similes. But these metaphors, too, never replace the needs of terms; similes and metaphors are in the philosophical systems mere illustrative additions or corroborations, never primary keywords in themselves, showing the direction towards which their doctrines tend. Secondarily, however, these pregnant metaphors, while adequately illuminating philosophical concepts, may gain the position of keywords.

---

5. I have dealt with the fully developed similes of Vedānta on p. 24-25.

As to the question of the Alaṅkāraśāstram and the significance of technical terms and compounds with prefixes within this system of Rhetoric, we have to start from the remark above that the Alaṅkāraśāstram is only a secondary system. As its very name suggests, it is only a systematic teaching of *Alaṅkāra*s which are adopted readymade, as it were, from poetry. As such, it is limited in its scope from the very outset. Furthermore, it has to deal with something which in itself is already limited by the poet's artistic aims. *Alaṅ-kāra* means literally — near to one of the meanings of *Saṁ-(s)kāra* — something which is (already) made suffcient and perfect, not containing possibilities for further potentialities. These very facts provide no fertile soil, so to speak, for the development of living technical terms as expressions of tendencies.

The Alaṅkāraśāstram is connected with Logic and Grammar (see above) and as such adapts logical terms to its special contents: *prati-bhā* designates the poet's inspiration; *vi-bhāvanā* is the imagination required from his audience; *vi-cheda* or *vi-chitti* is artistic subtlety; *pari-kara* is indirect (*pari*: round-about) intimation; *sā-hitya* is poetical composition; *rūpaka* is metaphor or dramatic composition; *dhvani* is suggested sense (like in Grammar), etc.

Even when the *Alaṅkāra*-system invents terms as means for technical classification these are merely "descriptive" terms, but not bearers of fertile postulates as the genuine terms in the philosophical systems are. Here are some examples : *apa-hnuti*, (apparent) negation; *nindā*, (apparent) blame; *pra-śaṁsā*, praise; *atiśaya-ukti*, hyperbolical expression; *pary-āya* (*ukti*), rhetorical detour, etc.

There is scarcely room in the Alaṅkāraśāstram for genuine simple terms; still less is there room for compound-terms in which prefixes indicate all the possibilities of potential and not yet attained aims.

6

A Countertest

Sanskrit Prefix-terms and their Western Equivalents or Counterparts

As a countertest for the preceding line of argument I add a short survey of technical terms formed with prefixes and their Western equivalents. A comparison between the Sanskrit terms and their rendering in European languages will throw into relief some further aspects of the difference in ways of thought between India and the West.

For the comparison I make use of those compound-terms only for which India and the West choose verbal roots of the same or similar meaning (it goes without saying that verbal roots taken from contradictory aspects would require contradictory prefixes and would thus not provide any basis of comparison).

There are some prefix-terms in Sanskrit philosophical terminology which are represented by terms with the same[1] Indo-European prefixes in the Western languages. Some others, too, take corresponding forms, if not literally, yet according to their contents. More instructive for our purpose, however, are those apparent equivalents in which the basic concepts of India and the West are fundamentally different. Either divergent aspects are expressed in the prefix-terms, or the equivalents in Western languages are given in simple terms and not in the

---

1. If not strictly philologically, then at any rate semasiologically.

dynamic form of prefix-terms (very rarely the opposite process can be traced that Sanskrit uses merely pregnant simple terms, while the Western languages apply a compound-term instead). Furthermore, Sanskrit philosophical terminology sometimes employs multiple prefixes, while the West is satisfied with the use of simple prefixes; this is because the latter is only concerned with stating the results, i.e. the static meaning of the term instead of illustrating also the dynamic process implied. In addition, Sanskrit terminology also forms terms with one or more prefixes which the Western languages, however, can only express through adding attributive appositions to the simple term. It is characteristic of Sanskrit syntax to accumulate compounds, while the Western structure prefers separate members of a sentence: noun and adjective, etc. The Sanskrit prefixes are, as claimed throughout the previous chapters, still sufficiently dynamic in meaning to show complicated and developing inter-relationship, not merely a piecing together of deadened isolated parts.

In confronting Sanskrit and Western terms one has to keep in mind some fundamental difficulties: once and for all, every translation is actually already an interpretation. Secondly, there is the fact that in both languages, Sanskrit and its Western equivalents, not only a single term but its possible synonyms have to be considered. Do not synonyms bring in already in one and the same language various aspects of the concept which we are trying to confront ?

The following exposition is not meant to do more than indicate a few leading ideas. Thus, I limit myself to a few examples and refer mostly to one European language only, i.e. English, which generally provides in its philosophical terminology survivals of Greek and Latin.

Of the first group of corresponding equivalents I may now give a few examples. The Sanskrit prefix *sam* is represented in

Greek by *syn*, in Latin by *con*, in German by *zusammen*, etc. Thus, *saṁ-varaṇa* corresponds to com-pression. German *Zusammen-fassung*. *Saṁ-sarga* is adequately rendered by contact; *saṁ-khyā* by com-putation; *saṁ-ghāta* by com-pilation. In these examples the prefixes are the same in Sanskrit and its equivalents and the nouns to which they are added are of similar meanings.

Sanskrit *pra* in one of its meanings corresponds to Latin *pro*: *pra-dhāna* means pro-minent; *pra-vac* and *pra-brū* find their equivalents in pro-claim, pro-nounce, and pro-pound. *Pra-vr̥tti* is adequately rendered as pro-cess. *Upa-grahaṇa*, *upa-labdhi*, and *upa-patti* correspond to German *Auf-fassung*.

This first group contains prefixes which are exactly the same[2] in Sanskrit and other Indo-European languages and accordingly represents terms which express the same concepts in India and the West, though their dynamic functions are still felt more vividly in Sanskrit than in their Western sister-languages.

A second set may be represented by terms in which Sanskrit applies prefixes which are linguistically different, but regularly analogous in meaning. The Sanskrit prefix *ati* finds its counterpart in Greek *hyper* and Latin *trans*; e.g. *ati-tarati* means trans-gress; *ati-śaya* is hyper-bole. *Adhi-sthā* is to super-intend. *Ā-krama* and *ā-pāta* find their equivalent in in-vasion, and *upa-cāra* and *ā-kṣepa* in al-lusion. *Nir-vāṇa* contains the same concept as de-struction; *niś-caya* and *ava-sāya* or *ava-dhāraṇā* denote decision. *Ava-tāra* is de-scent; *apa-varga* is de-liverance. The Latin prefix *de* corresponds to more than one Sanskrit prefix.

On the other hand, some of the Sanskrit prefixes are in the West represented by a number of different prefixes; especially is this the case with the prefixes *prati* and *vi*. *Prati-*

2. If not strictly philologically, then at any rate semasiologically.

pakṣin is op-ponent; *prati-yoga* and *prati-ṣṭhāna* is counter-part or German: *Gegen-stand. Prati-bandh* is inter-cept; *prati-jñā* is as-sertion. In other cases *prati* is represented by the Latin *re-;* e.g. *prati-bimb, prati-bhā,* and *prati-kṣip;* re-flect; *prati-bhāṣ* is re-spond. *Vi-śeṣa* denotes di-stinction or dif-ference. *Vy-akta* corresponds to e-manated, while *vi-bhu* finds its adequate rendering in per-vading. *Vi-tarka* is de-composing (ana-lysis).

A difference in the dynamics, but not in the basic concept of Sanskrit and Western terms may be pointed out in yet another group. The Sanskrit terms use, for instance, two similar prefixes which corroborate each other, while the Western languages, in a less dynamic manner, employ only one: *up*(*a*)-*ā-dhi* is at-tribution; *adhy-ā-ropa* is ap-plication; *praty-abhi-jñā* is re-cognition; *praty-ā-satti* is ana-logy; *abhy-upa-gama* is ac-ceptance; *vy-ut-thāna* is a-scending; here the function of e-levation is expressed in the horizontal direction by *vi* and vertically by *ut. Saṁ-ni-pāta* is accordingly con-nection emphasized in Sanskrit in the horizontal direction (*sam*) and in the vertical sphere (*ni*) as well.

Another group of terms formed in Sanskrit with double prefixes and expressed in Western languages by only one prefix, agree with their Western equivalents in the result; but the Sanskrit term significantly illustrates the dynamic approach to this result as well in adding yet another prefix. For instance, *adhy-ava-sāya* is de-cision; *sam-ā-dhi* is con-centration; *vy-abhi-cāra* is de-viation; *sam-ā-patti* and *sam-ā-gama* is con-nection. *Vy-ati-ṣaṅga, vy-ati-kara* and *vy-ati-hāra* are pregnant terms denoting ex-change. *Praty-ava-marśa* is re-flection. Sometimes not only two but even three prefixes are applied in Sanskrit to illustrate all stages of the process together with its result: *prati-sam-ā-dhā* is re-dress. This accumulation of prefixes is preferably used when the term bears on complicated logical processes: *abhi-vy-ā-haraṇa* means de-signation.

Somewhat different nuances are represented by those Sanskrit terms which depict both process and result, while the Western equivalent demonstrates the process only: *upa-saṁ-krama* and *upa-saṁ-pāda* mean: ar-rival; *vi-prati-kāra* is counter-action; suggesting by the prefix *vi* that not only the counter-motion, but its result, the dis-sension, is also taken into consideration.

An instructive example of similar tendency but reversed expression may also be added. In *pra-saṅga*, con-sequence, the meanings of prefix and verbal root are crosswise exchanged in Sanskrit and in its Western equivalents. The root *sañj*, to stick together, finds its equivalent in the Latin prefix *con*, while the forward movement is illustrated by the Sanskrit prefix *pra* and in the Latin verbal noun respectively.

Sometimes the less dynamic thinking of the West is satisfied with a plain simple term where the dynamic way of India needs prefixes for expressing the process. *Saṁ-jñāna* and *vi-jñāna* are simply rendered by: knowledge, while the prefix *sam* indicates the synthetic and the prefix *vi* the analytic way of reaching this knowledge. *Ava-sthā* is: status; when applying the same verbal noun in Sanskrit and Latin (*sthā*, respectively *sta*) one finds in Sanskrit a more illustrative designation by means of the added prefix *ava*, fixing downward. *Vi-sarga*, creation, indicates in Sanskrit the di-spersing function (*vi*) of emanation. *Ava-graha*, Space, underlines the locative sense by supplementing the prefix *ava*. *Ā-kāśa*, ether, is shown in its function of spreading forth (*ā*) light; *ni-yama*, logical rule, is made pregnant in its fixation by the prefix *ni*, downward. *Ānv-īkṣikī*, philosophy, shows the function of surveying; the tendency towards a generalizing knowledge seems to be more strongly expressed by the prefix than by the Greek *philo*, though its literal translation is loving. . .

Double prefixes, too, are applied where Western languages use simple nouns which do not illustrate the function. *Vy-ut-patti* means etymology; grammar (or ana-lysis) is pregnantly expressed in Sanskrit by a term with two prefixes: *vy-ā-karaṇa*. *Upa-ni-ṣad*, an apparently deadened *nomen proprium* for a group of Vedānta texts, shows in its very prefixes the approach and settling down with a teacher to indicate the eagerness of the pupil and his determination of a continuous study.[3]

Very seldom, indeed, can the reverse process be traced that Sanskrit applies a simple term and the West indicates the function by a prefix-term: *javana* and *codanā* are considered as verbal nouns pregnant enough to denote im-pulse. Mostly, however, even when the Sanskrit verbal root would alone be sufficiently dynamic in meaning, a prefix is still added for further emphasis: *khāta*, dug-out or up-rooted, is frequently found in the form *ut-khāta* (lit. dug-out-out).

In some cases when India and the West are using fundamentally the same concept the Western languages have to add an attributive adjective to do justice to the full concept which Sanskrit can express sufficiently by prefixes. Here are some examples: *vy-ā-moha* and *saṁ-moha*, complete confusion; *anu-vy-ava-sāya*, secondary cognition; *vi-prati-patti*, mutual discrepancy; *saṁ-prati-patti*, general concept; *abhi-pra-ṇaya*, firm devotion; *saṁ-pari-ṣvakta*, completely embracing; *nir-vy-ūḍha*, fully demonstrated; *sam-ā-patti*, all-attainment. *Vi-pary-āya* is: erroneous view; *vi-praty-aya* is: confused concept; *vy-apa-deśa* and *vy-ā-khyā* is: detailed assertion and explanation; *vi-pra-laya* is: complete dissolution. *Abhi-vy-añjana* is: distinctive and intentional manifestation; *nir-vi-cikitsā* and *nir-vi-cāra* is: definite

3. For the above interpretation cf. Śaṅkara's remarks of *upāsana* to *Taitt. Up.* Śikṣādhyāya, 3, 4, and 12, 1. For further instances of *upa-sad* and *up(a)-ās* see my review of E. Senart, "Bṛhadāraṇyaka Upaniṣad," *J.R.A.S.*, 1937, pp. 501ff.

settlement; *praty-ava-marśa* is: profound deliberation or meditation. The Western attributive adjective is an *external* closer definition, while in Sanskrit a further *immanent* variation of the process is expressed by prefixes.

The translations of some terms have to have adjectives added to them to suggest the full meaning which is already implicit in the original Sanskrit prefix-term. The individual *Ātman* is illustrated in his quality of being a reflection of the universal *Ātman* by his designation as *praty-ag-Ātman*. *Prat(y)-ītya-sam-ut-pāda* is a term expressed by the dynamics of three prefixes and one verbal absolutive mood (*itya*) which requires an abstract nominal rendering with descriptive attributes. As such, it is void of its concrete functional meaning in the translation: mutual dependency.

Sometimes the rendering of a Sanskrit prefix-term requires in the West not only a corresponding prefix, but a closer definition as well, because the original sense of the prefix was forgotten in its Western equivalent. Thus, *ā-deśa* means : an in-dication which is vague and general (to illustrate the vague and general forward motion implied in *ā*).

But the distinction between the mentality of India and the West may even go so far that not only dynamics but also the underlying concepts expressed by prefix and noun are distinctly different. *Ā-lambana*, *ā-yatana* and *ā-śraya*, all indicate an active tendency towards a hold which is to be found; they are represented in the West by sup-port which stresses the passive expectation of an aid from without (German: unter die Arme greifen).[4] However, there are some terms, especially those of epistemology, where a greater activity is significantly mirrored in the Western term. Ap-prehension is a stronger

4. One may view these Sanskrit terms with regard to the fundamental Indian concept of self-activity in gaining Liberation.

expression of intentional approach than its sanskrit equivalent *anu-bhava*, which indicates a receptive adaptation. *Praty-aya* and *prati-patti* are, like *prati-bimba*, knowledge in the sense of mechanical re-flection; *aut-pattika* is a quasi-mechanical spontaneous pro-duction. The same holds good for the Western term *ob-struction*, *ob* being an Indo-European equivalent of Sanskrit *abhi*. Ob-struction designates the meaning of counter-function, while its Sanskrit equivalent *ni-rodha* illustrates a mere passivity, the downwards direction of compressing without counter-pressure.

On the other hand, there are some terms of Indian logic in which a greater activity is expressed in the Sanskrit concept than in its Western equivalent. *Upa-naya* and *nir-ṇaya* depict con-clusion; *ni-gamana* and *ny-āya* also are less static designations for the same Western concept. Similarly, *upa-cāra* and *upa-māna* are dynamic expressions for com-parison. But it is noteworthy that a greater activity expressed by a Sanskrit logical term can only be traced when it is not the subjective dominant attitude of human reasoning but only an objective eagerness of approach that is suggested. *Pari-bhāṣā* and its equivalent "de-finition" once more reveal a difference of attitude between India and the West; while the West masterfully de-fines, the Indian thinker humbly and objectively encircles his object by viewing it from all possible angles. *Par(y)-īkṣā*, the look around the thing, means to in-vestigate it, i.e. to pursue it. *Saṁ-jñā*, de-signation, is for the Indian thinker, as the prefix *sam* suggests, an act of gathering together the knowledge; de-signation, on the other hand, denotes the tendency of singling out certain characteristics. *Saṁ-vāda*, dis-cussion or dia-logue, too, reflect the Indian generalizing, the Western separating, tendency for the attainment of knowledge. Only the Latin equivalent *col-loquium* comes near to the attitude revealed by the Sanskrit term.

Fundamentally different concepts can be traced in Sanskrit terms of Eschatology and their Western renderings. *Saṁ-sāra* is translated as : trans-migration or re-birth; but the Sanskrit prefix *sam* indicates a comprehensive view on the whole interconnected series of incarnations, while the West only states one single phase of the process. Instructive, too, are the Sanskrit terms *pra-yāta* and *pra-ita*; they are generally translated as "deceased". Deceased and German *ab-scheiden* indicate the separation from the body or from the world in the moment of death, while *pra-yāta* and *pra-ita* denote an intentional forward motion (*pra*) to a further state of development by means of the transition into death.

And now a final word on the question of synonyms. One may object that all translations are interpretations only and as such bound to be controversial. Can we really, then, grasp the one adequate equivalent? A further objection may be raised that in one and the same language there are always synonyms at hand to express the same or a similar concept. As to the first question of translation or interpretation some kind of test must lie in the linguistic feeling of the translator himself.

A few words may be added with regard to the second question, that of synonyms. On the whole, all synonyms cover the same or a similar concept; but one may point out three different ways by which synonyms are gained in Sanskrit terminology. First, the same prefixes are applied and the change in the term comes in only through the application of synonymous verbal roots; for instance, the term dis-union is in Sanskrit expressed either by *vi-(pra) yoga* or by *vi-śleṣa, śliṣ* and *yuj* having a similar meaning. The function of the prefix, which, in all the synonyms, is equally employed, generally is so strong that it unifies, as it were, the different meanings of the verbal noun to which it is attached. This law holds good not only for the synonyms within Sanskrit, but also in a way for the Sanskrit term and its Western equivalents in general.

There are two Sanskrit terms for doubt: *saṁ-śaya* and *saṁ-deha* lying together and being confused with each other. *Vi-veka, vi-cāraṇa* and *vi-marśa,* all mean discrimination as result of consideration.

But besides these synonyms which are homogeneous in meaning through the application of the same prefix, there are other synonyms bearing on the same concepts which are viewed from quite another aspect and are thus formed with other prefixes also. To the group of synonyms for doubt (*saṁ-śaya* and *saṁ-deha*) belongs also *ā-śaṅkā. Śaṅkā* alone as a simple term designates already doubt, but it is dynamically emphasized by the prefix *ā*. Doubt is thus viewed in its seeking of a way-out and not only expressed by the static statement of the different possibilities lying together. As to the set of the synonyms indicating contemplation or consideration which significantly is in Sanskrit primarily seen not from its aspect of lying together (*con*), but in the proceeding stages of dis-cernment (*vi*), there are still other synonyms which grasp the same concept at a later stage. *Ava-loka* and *ā-locanā* are also synonyms for consideration after dis-cernment. The term *ava-loka* expresses that a survey is taken from above, while *ā-locanā* suggests that the view of the subject in question is kept in the forward direction(*ā*), so as to reach the desired mental result.

A slightly different tinge is found in terms like *anv-aya* and *saṁ-bandha,* which both mean con-text. *Anu* and *sam* are both working on the horizontal line, but according to the tendencies of the prefixes applied these synonyms indicate different functions. *Anv-aya* expresses a relation between the different members of the sentence in the sense of an adaptation of one to another; *saṁ-bandha,* on the other hand, depicts like its Western equivalent "con-text" a quasi-external connection of parts.

Different verbal roots and different prefixes, i.e. altogether different viewpoints, are illustrated in still another way of forming synonyms. Di(s)-stinction is expressed in Sanskrit by *pari-cheda* and *vi-śeṣa; pari-chid* means : to encircle the object under investigation and thus to cut it off (*cheda*), while its synonym *vi-śeṣa* suggests, nearer to its Western equivalent, a function of singling out the object, so that it remains apart. The logical function of concluding and inferring too, finds in Sanskrit different synonyms formed with different verbs and prefixes; it thus reflects different approaches. *Anu-māna* is measuring along; *ava-sāna* is fastening down; *upa-saṁ-hāra* is tending towards (*upa*) and collecting (*sam*) the necessary instances; the further synonyms *niś-caya* and *nir-ṇaya* illustrate both the function of de-composing or de-ducing as necessary steps towards the result, the conclusion.

Different aspects of "duty" are mirrored in the different prefixes and their respective verbal roots used in Sanskrit. Besides the expressive but ambiguous simple term *dharma* duty is designated by *ni-yama; adhi-kāra; anu-ṣṭheya,* and *vi-dhi. Ni-yama* depicts the restraint, the controlling function of duty; *adhi-kāra* expresses the impetus of fulfilling, or the submission to, a duty; *anu-ṣṭheya* shows the path we have to follow in duty and *vi-dhi* the different (*vi*) statutes implied in duty.

The same variety of approach is expressed in the synonyms for "teacher". Besides the simple term *guru,* the weighty one, we find prefixed terms like *ā-cārya,* one who is to be approached (from the pupil); *upa-deśaka,* he who is capable of providing information, and *up(a)-ādhy-āya,* he who knows the things thoroughly after having approached them on different ways (*upa* and *adhi*).

This basic comparison and confrontation with the West is not impaired by the fact that one concept can be expressed by different synonyms, even in Sanskrit itself. On the contrary, through the very study of Sanskrit synonymous terms one can reach yet another distinction between India and the West. Synonyms are the expression of India's thinking. The predilection for forming synonyms is based on India's love of paraphrase instead of clear-cut, one-sided designation. The meaning required is gathered from various approaches, from all possible aspects.

Prefixes are the protagonists in the dramatic play, as it were, of synonymous ambiguities. Synonyms are formed either by the means of the same predominant prefix which instils, so to speak, its tendency into several more or less verbal roots or else by means of different prefixes which suggest divergent functions and approaches from different sides.

Each prefix-term, and still more each group of prefix-terms, teaches that India has retained and developed in all detailed subtlety a dynamic mode of expression which is unequalled in any language of the West.[5]

London, 1945 Betty Heimann
Revised, London, 1950

5. While finishing this study on Prefixes the graphic pregnancy of prefixes became so evident to me that I ventured to present their dynamics and characteristic motions in linear charts which I used in my classes at the University of Ceylon. These diagrams of prefixes together with other illustrations of Hindu philosophical notions I hope shortly to publish as "Hindu Thought in Illustration" (about 60 charts to which short explanatory captions are added).

Index of Terms Treated